The Newly-Made Mason

By H.L. Haywood
Revised by Michael R. Poll

A Cornerstone Book

The Newly-Made Mason
By H.L. Haywood
Revised by Michael R. Poll

A Cornerstone Book
Published by Cornerstone Book Publishers
An Imprint of Michael Poll Publishing

Cornerstone Book Publishers
Hot Springs Village, AR

First Cornerstone Edition - 2010
Second Cornerstone Edition - 2020
Third Revised Cornerstone Edition - 2023

www.cornerstonepublishers.com

ISBN: 9781613424001

TABLE OF CONTENTS

PREFACE

The fraternity of Freemasons is ancient and worldwide. In it are many men who did not stop with reading one or two books about it but have read countless numbers and have given to its scholarship all the years of their lives. They are veterans of Masonic study who know it within and without. Their knowledge is to other men as an ocean is to a creek. If they were to sit together as a senate, and if a Newly-Made Mason were to go to them when he seeks those "well-informed brethren" whom the ritual bids him to seek, they would give him the same counsel which well-informed brethren anywhere would give him, except that they would go one step further. In their considerable knowledge of the history of the Craft they have learned how easily Masons can twist a proper understanding of Freemasonry or miss it. They would remind him that he has a responsibility not to misrepresent to his mind the Masonry to which he has committed himself. They would urge him to give to his own thinking about it the same "square work" and "true work" which he gives to his duties on the floor of his lodge. It is possible that they would therefore ask him to pledge himself in a second obligation, which might read in some such form as this:

> "I hereby solemnly and sincerely promise and swear that as a beginning Craftsman in the Masonry of the mind and as a Newly-Made Mason, I will not permit myself to be led into making hasty conclusions. I promise and swear that I will not listen to those who are not competent to teach me. There will be nothing binding on me except the truth. If some say one thing and others say the opposite thing, I will consider that it is Freemasonry

> that finally decides between them. We do not make the truth. We find the truth.
>
> "I furthermore promise and swear that I will never do violence to knowledge because there is nothing more sacred than a fact. I finally promise and swear that I will never permit either myself or any other by sophistry or ignorance, plausible cynicism or specious skepticism, to bring Freemasonry into doubt or dispute because I know it to be truthful and honorable."

I hope the reader of these chapters has already taken that obligation, at least in his heart, because these chapters have been written in that spirit. If there is something new in them, and possibly not said before in other Masonic books, it is not because the facts are new but because I have stated them in my own way. Some of the early chapters are epitomes of the more fundamental periods in the history of Freemasonry and answer the question: "How did lodges come to exist?" Chapters on the organization, constitutions, and laws of the lodge follow in due order, as do chapters also, in another series, on the work done by the lodge, including the Ritual and Symbols. The teachings and ideas incorporated in the work are explained one after another in the ensuing groups of chapters. Though each is complete and may be read without reference to the others, they are bound together by a single purpose: to describe and explain the work of the Craft so that a Newly-Made Mason can see it steadily and see it.

It is an old custom to dedicate a book to a friend, to a sponsor, to a helper, to the memory of a brother. I am writing the dedication of this book into this Preface instead of presenting it separately because the dedication is the truest Preface to the book. Theodore Sutton Parvin, one-time Grand Secretary of Iowa, founded and fathered the Iowa Masonic Library, the world's largest collection of

Masonic books. Many years ago, his son and successor, Newton R. Parvin, also Grand Secretary and Grand Librarian, made me feel as free to use the contents of those thousand shelves as if I had owned them myself. When he, in turn, was followed by his successor, Charles C. Hunt, the latter continued with equal generosity, the same courtesies, and this book is hereby dedicated to them. If in the limitless fields of Masonic study, to use Frederick Meyer's words, these chapters "draw a little closer to that which is infinitely far," it is because that library and these three brethren made it possible.

H. L. Haywood

FOREWORD TO THE CORNERSTONE EDITION

Not long ago, a young man turned in his petition to a Masonic lodge. Maybe a relative of his was a Mason, or maybe, he learned of Freemasonry from a popular book or movie. Regardless, he expressed his desire to join.

A few weeks after turning in his petition, he received a phone call from a man who told him he was a member of an investigation committee working on the petition. He asked the young man if he and two other lodge members could come to his house to meet with him. They met at the appointed time. It was a good meeting. Questions were asked, and everyone learned a bit more about each other.

The committee told the young man that Freemasonry is not an insurance agency. While lodges and individual Masons have a long and honorable history of assisting those in need, Freemasonry is not designed to be a charitable organization like the Red Cross.

Freemasonry is also not a civic association such as the Jaycees or Lions Club. The primary goal of Freemasonry is to take good men and, through moral instruction, give them the keys by which they can, hopefully, make themselves better and happier in their lives.

The young man took in all that he was told. He then asked about the history of Freemasonry. He was told we don't have a complete or clear understanding of our beginnings. We know that we are old. As an organization, we go back to around 1717 with the reported creation of the Grand Lodge of England. But many claim that we can trace ourselves to much earlier times — to the days of the old Operative Freemasons. Many also claim that we can trace our philosophy and manner of symbolic education to an even much earlier time. Sadly, we just don't have definitive answers. The young petitioner accepted everything he was told, and the committee left. Both sides were satisfied.

The young man was quietly excited. He knew that what he wanted to join was very old and important. He couldn't explain why, but he felt it deep in his heart. He had done his homework. He had already read many of the popular books and conducted internet searches of Freemasonry. He knew better than to pay attention to the large amount of flash concerning Freemasonry. He ignored the wild supernatural claims and nonsensical satanic charges. But he knew there was something uniquely special about Freemasonry, its manner of instruction by degrees, and the whole Masonic philosophy. He felt excited about joining.

In a few weeks, a letter told him that the lodge had voted on his petition. The ballot was clear, and the date of the initiation was set. But there were many questions that he had forgotten to ask. One thing that he was unsure about was how he should dress for the initiation. He thought about calling but then remembered some of the books he owned and how the Masons wore business suits, and some even wore tuxedoes. The photos were not all that old, so he thought he should try to match their dress. He knew this was something special but assumed they would have told him if they wanted him to wear a tux. So, he decided to wear his suit.

When he showed up at the lodge, some members were wearing old blue jeans and equally faded and worn polo shirts — some sported t-shirts. Others looked like they were wearing soiled work clothes and had come directly to the lodge from work. He felt a bit out of place in such a casual atmosphere. One of the men laughed when he saw him and asked if he was going to church or a wedding.

The young man waited downstairs and was finally called up for the initiation. He felt slightly uncomfortable as the man who came down for him laughed and said,

"Now, you are in for it!" In for what? What did he mean by that?

He was placed in a little room by a kindly elderly man who seemed sincerely interested in his well-being. This made him feel better. The degree began.

After the degree ended, the young man had mixed emotions. He knew what he had experienced was extremely significant, but why was so much laughter and talking going on? Why did he hear a considerable amount of yelling out of instructions? It was clear that some who spoke did not, at all, know their lines (they were stumbling and fumbling over every few words), and others, from everywhere, were telling the officers what to say (and loudly).

While walking around, he also heard about someone's wife being sick and another's cousin building a new garage. What did all that have to do with his degree? But, afterward, everyone was so friendly. Maybe he expected too much. Maybe Freemasonry is just a group of men who meet to enjoy themselves and try to do antiquated and meaningless rituals now and then.

In time, the young man's feelings about Masonry changed from before his joining. These were all nice guys. Every time he went to a meeting, he was greeted with smiles, friendly handshakes, and inquiries about his health and well-being.

There was a mixture of blue collars workers and professional men. All seemed genuinely interested in the lodge, but most could not answer even the basic questions concerning Freemasonry. It was almost as if Freemasonry and the lodge were two completely different things. Questions on the ritual or history were always passed to one brother, who they said was the "answer man." They were a nice group of men – friends – but there was nothing *special* in the lodge, special in the way he viewed Masonry before he joined. This was a club made up of good guys who would meet a couple of times a month to enjoy themselves. They would visit and share a few laughs during a friendly evening. That seemed to be all that he could expect from the lodge experience. The books clearly were speaking of something else. But what? Who were the Freemasons he had read about? Did they ever exist? Was it all made up to sell books?

After a few months, the young man found that a TV show was scheduled at the same time as his lodge meeting. It was a show that he had wanted to watch for some time. He chose the show over the lodge. Over the next few months and years, it became easier and easier to choose many events over the lodge meetings.

Eventually, the young man attended the lodge, maybe, once or twice a year. He made an effort to try to attend some of the important meetings. He did so out of a feeling of obligation, not enjoyment. He did see some who truly seemed to enjoy each and every meeting. These were the men who kept the lodge alive.

At a few meetings, some who were always there gently scolded him for not attending more lodge functions. "You know, the lodge depends on its members, and if you don't support the lodge, it will fail." But what was he to do? Was he really obligated to continually go to a place that provided him with no benefit at all other than a few laughs and a meal? He had tried, but after months of only hearing a reading of the minutes of the last meeting, bills that needed to be paid, who was sick, and discussion of the next planned social event, he grew disinterested. He knew that he could spend his time in more productive ways.

So, was he to be blamed as it was suggested? He even read such things from "ranking" Masons, who seemed to put all responsibility for the success or failure of a body on his simply attending, regardless of what was offered. The man at the top was never to blame, and even if he was, nothing was ever done. There was no accountability for poor leadership. It was always the rank-and-file members who seemed to be the responsible parties.

The suggestion was that there was some lacking in the young Mason, and he needed to "wake up" and give his total support to whatever was offered. Was there a lacking in him?

Clearly, Freemasonry either failed this young man in about every way possible, or there truly was some lacking in him, or a misunderstanding on his part as to the actual nature of Freemasonry. Is Freemasonry only a club of good men who try to do charitable work and hold friendly meetings, or is it an organization designed to educate and uplift its members through moral instruction? And, where was such instruction?

In several publications, the young man saw it written: "Freemasonry is the world's oldest and largest fraternity. Its history and tradition date to antiquity. Its singular purpose is to make good men better." OK, that's clear. But how do we do that?

Since this quote was written in a Masonic education publication, maybe that should give us a clue. We should teach and instruct our candidates. There are countless books and articles written on Masonic education. We learn the importance of education and teaching in our very ritual. But, apart from the ritual, do we actually *teach* Freemasonry, or is it only words to be spoken or read and not acted upon? How many young men are lost to us because we fail to do what we say we will do?

William Lowe Bryan (the 10th president of Indiana University) is credited with writing: "Education is one of the few things a person is willing to pay for and not get." I believe this is sometimes spot-on regarding Freemasonry (and has been for many years). I believe the hole left when quality education ceased in the lodges may have been replaced with additional fellowship. That's not a bad thing, but it's not the lifeblood of Freemasonry. Initiation and making good men "better" are our main reasons for existence.

The passing of time is unavoidable. Every year, our lodges hold elections for officers to lead them for the next year. The young men who came into the lodge, but learned little about Freemasonry, are now in leadership positions. They are the leaders, but truthfully, many are not qualified. To be fair, it's not their fault. With the speed many of them go through the chairs, how can they help but be inexperienced? They are where they are because someone tapped them on the shoulder and asked them if they would accept a position. They were just trying to be helpful.

Maybe the lodge felt it had no one else to ask and had to take whoever it could to "sit in the chair." Maybe it was felt that to take anyone, even someone very inexperienced, was better than closing shop. Where Masonic education once took place, discussions of lodge picnics or other lodge events are heard at the meetings. The time that the Worshipful Master once spent on planning the Masonic education of the members is often now spent on trying to learn the basics of lodge leadership.

Lodge meetings are only as long as felt necessary, and then the "enjoyable" time of the lodge takes place – sharing a few laughs with friends. The leaders are expected to keep the members happy, not spend too much money and get through their year with as little hassle as possible. The "hole" was filled, and we are marking time, just getting through the years.

But, marking time and just getting by does not secure the future of Freemasonry. It is not responsible. It is not enough to *say* we are "Freemasonry," but act like a club. We must either be what we say or admit to being something else.

To all the junior officers of Freemasonry, no matter if you are brand new to Freemasonry or have been a Mason for many years and are only now returning to lodge activity, no matter what level of experience and knowledge you have — *stop*. Take a breath. You are not alone. You don't have to have a situation where young men leave your lodges because of claims that you are not giving them what they expected. You don't have to worry that you will suddenly be in charge and not know what in the world to do or say. You have Brothers who wish to help you.

But, just as each of you had to step up and ask to join Freemasonry, you must make your needs and desires known. And, when you are a junior officer is the time when you should do this.

The internet is filled with Masonic education websites, but which are reliable? You may wish to seek out recognized and respected Masonic education sources. In the U.S., quality Masonic educational/service societies which you can and should join, such as The Masonic Service Association of North America, and other worthy state and national organizations, are designed to provide quality Masonic educational resources and services.

I believe deeply in the importance of finding balance in everything. Going too far one way or the other never seems to bring about what is truly desired. But what do we do about our present situation? We have already gone too far. Our lodges have taken on more of the appearance of clubs than lodges of moral instruction. It was not done through maliciousness but out of a desire to help and preserve. It did not happen all at once but over a period of time. It was done with no ill intentions. We all know that there is a problem in our lodges. We know that they are not the same lodges as before.

We hear the stories of days long gone. Our leaders desire to do good, but some are uncertain about the best path. None wish for everything to fall apart on their watch. Some may feel that doing nothing is better than doing the wrong thing. But cancer is never cured by inaction. There is an old Rosicrucian thought that everything felt to be of value must face the test of death. What is truly of value will come back alive. What is of no value will fade away. Is Freemasonry of value?

I do not believe that society (or any group of people) is changed in mass by outside stimuli. I believe that change always comes through individual change. When we change as individuals, and if others change in a like manner, then society changes. I believe the first step we can take is to recognize that we are in trouble and traveling in the wrong direction. Value is a perception. We place whatever value we choose on something. Value can also change. If you don't treat something as special or valuable, it's not.

Anyone who knows me personally knows that I live in blue jeans. But those who only know me from lodge believe I live in business suits. Going to the lodge is something special to me. I dress accordingly. If I did not own a suit, I would clean myself and wear the best shirt and slacks I owned.

Try this the next time you visit your lodge: act as if it is a *very* special occasion, as if you are going to a *very* special place to do *very* special things. Do what you would do if you were going to such a special event.

Fix your mind to always treat going to the lodge as important and special. Make that one permanent change in your life. After doing this, join or take advantage of what is offered in one of the Masonic education services or societies mentioned earlier.

Read the pages of this book. Study them. Read them again. Freemasonry will be what its members make it. The true and sole power within Freemasonry is where it has always been, with its members — with you.

Michael R. Poll
Cornerstone Book Publishers

Part One

Chapter I
Operative Freemasonry

The word "Mason" was the name of a workman in the building Craft in the Middle Ages. In England, that Craft was divided into five or six branches, called by different names, such as tilers, quarrymen, wallers, setters, etc., and each one of these was separately organized with its own officers, rules, and regulations; in the large centers of population they were organized as Masons' Companies, each with a building of its own, and working under the borough (municipal) ordinances which governed Companies of all the trades, arts, and professions. These branches and companies were a part of the general guild system in which the whole of Medieval work and trade was organized, and which was governed as a whole by a large body of guild laws; these laws belonged to the Law of the Realm, and since there was also in operation a body of laws enforced by the church, of authority equal to that of the state, and called The Ordinances of Religion, each guild was under a triple government: its own rules and regulations; civil laws; church laws. If any Craft preserved some custom, rule, or symbol, and if it continues to be in use, it does not follow that it had its origin in some practice in the work of the guild but may have been a church practice or a practice required by the civil law.

Among the five or six branches of the General Craft of Builders was one which confined itself to architecture properly so called, which is listed among the fine arts, and the practice of which is a profession. This branch belonged to the guild system in the sense that it came under general guild laws, but in a narrower sense was not a guild but was a fraternity; because after a member of it had finished his work in one place, he moved on to another, sometimes from one country to another. The Craftsmen in this Fraternity were called Freemasons. It was from this particular branch, and not from the building craft in general, that our own unique Fraternity of Freemasons descended. As a convenience, and to distinguish the first half of Masonic history from its later half, we call the workmen in the first period Operative Freemasons. In the later period, Speculative (or Accepted or non-Operative) Freemasons, but this distinction must not be pushed very far because, as we have learned from the past half-century of historical research, there is not as much difference between Speculative and Operative as we once believed; in Freemasonry, as a fraternity, there has been an unbroken continuity from the end of the Dark Ages (about the 10th Century) to the present time.

In order to make our history yet more intelligible, we must carry the distinction between the Freemason's branch of the early building craft and other branches to a further point. In the 14th Century, a number of Freemasons (though not all of them) began to organize permanent lodges. After that date, any given Freemason might or might not belong to one of those lodges. A further step came when among the two or three hundred lodges in Britain, a few of them in London set up a Grand Lodge in 1717. Each and every recognized lodge or Grand Lodge now in the world traces its history to that Grand Lodge. The line of our history can therefore be drawn from the general Craft of Masonry (or building) at the end of the Dark Ages, through the branch of it called Freemasonry, through the permanent lodges first set up among Freemasons in the 14th Century, through the Grand Lodge set up in 1717, by a few of those permanent lodges. We came from Medieval Operative Masonry, but we came from it along a particular path; in each year since the beginning, large areas of the building craft have remained outside the area which that path has traversed.

Architects were called Freemasons rather than Masons partly because they were in a fraternity and free to move about, partly because they worked in free-stone, and partly for a number of other and lesser reasons. The word "Freemason," in itself, can tell us little about our history. These Freemasons designed and constructed the cathedrals, churches, chapels, monasteries, nunneries, palaces, guildhalls, borough halls, college buildings, forts, and other structures of a monumental type. They were for public purposes, which then as now, stand far apart, almost in another world, from the simple structures of residences, stores, factories, barns, etc., which any man with ordinary skill and a few years of experience can learn to design and construct. The Freemasons were in a class apart from other Masons because their buildings were apart from others.

But it was not this superiority of the art of architecture to other building construction that gave Freemasons their great preeminence in the Middle Ages. There was the general illiteracy of the people during the long period between the end of the Dark Ages and the Reformation. The sciences were forbidden, and architecture was the only art to reach greatness. Next to the church itself, it accomplished more to shape the world during the Middle Ages than any other agency – even now, the Middle Ages are often represented or typified by a picture of a cathedral. Freemasons were, back then, what specialists in the pure sciences are today. They were selected men of extraordinary ability and talents. They were given long and strict training and education in a system of apprenticeship, and they each had to be equally adept in engineering, geometry, building design, carving, ornamentation, and sculpture. They had to be masters in the use of stone, that grandest and most difficult of all the materials with which men have ever had to work. The structures which they designed and constructed were not only for public use but also in their design and ornamentation had to express the spirit and ideas of religion, government, education, and society. It was also insisted that they be of high moral character. The Freemasons built at the center of those realms of culture because their work carried them there. For over two centuries, they were the supreme men in Britain and Europe for their intelligence, knowledge, ability, and character. No other society can look back to an ancestry nobler than our own.

Our pride in that ancestry could have been almost as great had the Operative Freemasons done nothing more than to carry on at an average level of excellence the old Roman architecture, called Romanesque, which they had recovered from the wreckage of the Dark Ages. But, in the 12th Century, they made a great discovery of their own which was so epoch-making that in the whole history of the world's architecture, only one other discovery (the Greek) could be compared with it. This was their invention of the extraordinary, radically new Gothic Style. It was this style which made the cathedrals possible (1,500 of them), and which, after it had percolated down to such details as the design of buttons and the shape of written letters of the alphabet, gave to Europe that shape, form, and color which in all cultural matters is meant by "Medieval." It called forth a Freemason who was a new kind of man, who mastered arts and sciences not known to others at the time, a man as great in mind as in skill. That particular development within the vast expanse of the building Craft, which finally led to our own fraternity, might have occurred if all architects for many generations had not been exclusively trained in the Gothic Style, but probably it would not have done so. Therefore 1140, the date of the very first Gothic building, is important in the history of Freemasonry.

The work of using a hammer and chisel on a block of stone was only one among many elements in the Fraternity of Freemasons. A Freemason had his family with him; if he had an apprentice, that apprentice was as much a part of his own family as a foster son; the families of the Freemasons at work in the same place were grouped together in a separate quarter or neighborhood. The Craftsmen at work, their lodge, and their neighborhood, along with everything belonging to each of them, comprised the Masonic Community. The rules and regulations, with the responsibilities of the Officers, included their Community and were not restricted to the lodge only. Apprentices had training, schooling, and education. Adult Craftsmen had to give as much time to thinking, studying, and designing as to work with their hands, for without geometry, engineering, and carving, they could do nothing. They were an organized community; therefore, there were Officers, meetings, and conferences. The Community had its own funds, religious observances, amusements, feasts, sports, and social life. It cared for its own injured, crippled, dead, widows, and orphans. In the meantime, the State and the Church were never far away, and civil laws and religious ordinances entered deeply into the Freemason's daily life to shape it in many ways. Much (and we might say "most") of what we now call Speculative Freemasonry was in the practice of the Fraternity eight centuries ago.

When a bishop decided to build a cathedral, he set up a board, usually with himself at its head, called an Administration or a Foundation. This board employed a Master of Masons who was a Freemason of high reputation, and after they had agreed with him on the general design of the building and costs, they and he together made a contract. He then sent out word for

Craftsmen. When a Craftsman applied, he identified himself, was examined, and if satisfactory, was "signed on," his family to follow. When a sufficient number were signed up, the Master called them together, and they formed themselves into a lodge, which continued to exist as long as the work was in progress and was dissolved when it was completed. The first act of the lodge was to secure housing for its members and their families; its next step was to erect a building for its use (sometimes two), which also was called the lodge. This building was the headquarters for daily work, a meeting place, and was also sometimes used as a work room. A *lodge* meant a body of Masons organized to work together as a unit. When the Master had instructions for all members, the lodge was called into *Communication*. The Freemasons worked according to a set of rules and regulations of their own, centuries old, among them being a number of Landmarks. Questions concerning the organization or work, as arose in any given lodge, were settled according to those rules. Since the same rules were in force wherever Freemasons worked, and each Apprentice and Fellow was under oath never to violate them, it was this body of rules which gave its unity and consistency to a Fraternity that had no national organization or officers and until the 12th Century did not even have permanent local organizations. At the same time, it preserved its rules and trade secrets to memory and taught them by word of mouth.

In that period, Freemasons had use of no books, handbooks, treatises, or blue-prints. So, anything they thought, learned, or put into practice which appeared to have permanent worth either had to be enacted on the floor of the lodge or else had to take an oral form. In order to preserve such things in their purity and to guard against alteration, these forms had to be repeated often. Such forms, thus repeated in exactly the same detail generation after generation, are what historians mean by *forms, ceremonies, and symbols.* If the word "symbolic" is used as a general name for the whole body of such fixed forms, then it is not an exaggeration to say that there was as much of this "Symbolic" Freemasonry in the earliest periods of the Operative Freemasonry as there is now in Speculative Freemasonry. And if we are willing to hazard an over-simplification, we also may say that if we grasp the eight or ten centuries of the history of Freemasonry as a whole, the only fundamental difference between Operative Masonry then and Speculative Masonry now is that a Speculative Freemason does not use Freemasonry as a means of livelihood, but for another purpose.

The 12th Century was the great formative period of the fraternity. Many existed and then died. If we look to see what *secret* was given to Freemasonry that allowed it to survive and grow while other guilds perished, the paragraphs above give us the answers. Whatever those Freemasons learned, which was to be preserved through future centuries, they learned in and from their work. Once they learned it, they did not put it into the form of abstract ideas, doctrines, or books (as we do) but incorporated it into their practices and customs. Instead of becoming a book, a lecture, or a creed, it became a ceremony, rite, or symbol. The Freemasons, as men of mind, stood far above the theologians, philosophers, and scholars of Britain for more than two centuries, and under "theologians" are included such men as Thomas Aquinas, Abelard, Roger Bacon, etc. What the theologians thought, they could write down in treatises; what the Freemasons thought, they embodied in their practices, customs, and symbols. Freemasons left the subject of theology to the theologians. They devoted their great minds to the great subject of their work. As will be explained in detail in later chapters, they were the first men in the world to discover the truth about the subject of that work. We modern Speculative Masons have, therefore, a double reason for looking back to the fathers and founders of our fraternity: we give them the veneration which men give everywhere to fathers and founders, and we look up to them, as also do historians of philosophy and theology, as having been great men of thought whose achievement as thinkers was even more epoch-making than their discovery of the Gothic Style in architecture. If they did not write down the new truths about work that they discovered in a book, it does not matter; any trained Mason can read the ritual as easily as an open book.

The Operative Period of Freemasonry was closed. Then came the Transition Period through a series of historical events which, by one of the most extraordinary coincidences known in history, occurred within a few years of each other. Henry VIII broke Great Britain's tie with the Pope and prepared the way for the Reformation. The same King also abolished the guild system – followed by the Mercantile System, a period in business and finance that present-day economics theorists find convenient to forget! The Renaissance broke into its final flower in the form of the printing press, with printed books, and changed the mental climate in Britain as much as in Europe generally. The discovery of America by Columbus opened the gates to the Age of Exploration, a wild and adventurous time in which Europe exploded over the world. Gothic architecture gave way with an almost abrupt suddenness to a new architectural style that originated in Italy and has since passed under many names, such as Classical, Neo-Classical, Italian, Palladian, and Wren. The old trade secrets of the Operative Freemasons could be kept secret no longer after *Euclid's Geometry* was published in print, along with many other lesser, old secrets in the arts and sciences. The center of control in Freemasonry passed from the individual Freemason going here and there in his work, and from his temporary lodges, into the permanent lodges which were constituted under the authority of manuscript copies of the Old Charges, and from them passed into the new Grand Lodge System after 1717.

CHAPTER II
YOU AND YOUR MASONRY

"Not more men in Masonry but more Masonry in men"

A non-Mason prays for the privileges and honors of membership by signing a *petition;* from the moment of signing, until he has received a favorable ballot, he is a *Petitioner*. From passing the ballot until he has been raised, he is a *Candidate*.

Initiation means "to be born into," and therefore, the *Three Degrees* taken together are an *Initiation* because they are how a Candidate is born into the world of Freemasonry. But it is more correctly used of the *Rite* by which he is made a member of a *Lodge of Entered Apprentices* (perhaps because of the verbal association of initiate with "initial" or first). A Candidate is said to be *Initiated as an Entered Apprentice, Passed to a Fellowcraft, and Raised a Master Mason*. In the United States, the *York Rite* is the rite used by most craft lodges.

Sanskrit was the ancient language from which both Greek and Latin originated. Since they are the mothers of modern European languages (with only two or three exceptions), Sanskrit is the mother of the majority of Occidental languages, including English. At least a hundred terms in Freemasonry are nothing but Sanskrit words, modified by usage (mother, father, brother, and sister are Sanskrit words). Ritual is one of these. In Sanskrit, it was "ri," and meant "to flow repetitively," hence it came to be the root of both "river" and rite. A *Rite* is a unique ceremony that moves forward in a series of waves (we may refer to them as "steps"), and the same ceremony is used over and over. The words "rhythm" and "rhyme" had a similar origin, and it is easy to see why. A ritual is a system of rites. The *Ritual of a lodge* of Ancient Craft Masonry is the system of the Three Degrees.

A symbol signifies or represents some truth, idea, fact, or teaching but is not itself the thing it represents; it may not even be similar. An emblem also represents or signifies something but is itself an instance of it. For example, a pen is an emblem of writing, and a sword is an emblem of war. An allegory is writing that tells a story. A lodge uses each of these for the stages of Initiation, Passing, and Raising. A single unit of writing and ceremonies is called a degree. The *Opening* and *Closing* of a lodge are called *Ceremonies*. The Ceremonies and Rituals of the lodge which are unlawful to write or publish is called the *Esoteric Work*; that which is published in official monitors is called the *Exoteric Work*.

The word *lodge* is of Anglo-Saxon origin and, in general use, has had at least fifteen separate meanings, of which some five or six are used in Freemasonry. Of these latter, the most important is as a chartered body of Masons and as the *Room* in which they meet. A local lodge is often called *constituent*. The sovereign body under which a lodge holds its charter is called a *Grand Lodge* – the "grand" signifying "head, or chief." The territory over which a lodge exercises authority is called its *jurisdiction*. A Grand Jurisdiction is the jurisdiction of a Grand Lodge. Any meeting of Masons presided over by Masonic officers is an Assembly. Assemblies fixed at regular times by the By-Laws for the transaction of lodge business are *Stated* or *Regular*. If called by the Worshipful Master, they are *Special* or *Emergent Communications*. The official written record of a Communication is called its *Minutes*.

In so far as Freemasonry consists of a body of Freemasons engaged in the same work, it is a *lodge*. As this work brings them into a personal association, it is a *Brotherhood*. Because its work is in order and its Officers have fixed positions and functions in this orderly work, it is an *Order*. Because they have a special friendliness for each other, and necessarily so, it is a *Fraternity*. Since it includes the relatives and friends of its members in its activities, it is a *Society*. And in respect of the fact that this society has its center in a building and therefore is in a neighborhood of its own, it is a *Masonic Community*.

The lodge officers, which are chosen by ballot, are said to be *Elective*; when named by the Worshipful Master, or other Lodge Officers, they are *Appointive*. Elective Officers have *Stations*; Appointive Officers have *Places*. Such Committees provided for by Grand Lodge law or the lodge By-Laws and are mandatory are said to be *Standing Committees*; *Special Committees* are appointed temporarily for particular purposes.

In no other Masonic field or subject is it as important to use technically correct terms as in *Masonic Jurisprudence*. It includes the laws, rules, and regulations according to which Masons govern themselves. Since these rules are unlike rules in other societies or fraternities, the terms used have specific Masonic definitions. The *Ancient Landmarks* are Freemasonry's fundamental laws, principles, and teachings. They may be written or printed but need not be, and neither gain nor lose when they are or are not. For that reason, they are all designated as *Unwritten Laws* — it would be even more correct to say that they are unwritable. A violation of a Landmark is called an *Innovation*.

A written instrument authorizing a group of Master Masons to constitute a lodge is usually called a *Dispensation*. Sometimes a Warrant and a lodge Under Dispensation are said to be *inchoate*, which means incomplete. The permanently written instrument under which a lodge works is called a *charter* — such a lodge is said to be *Duly Constituted*. A Regular Grand Lodge is one acknowledged, accepted, and recognized as a lawful Grand Body. A Regular lodge is a lodge on the chartered

List of a Regular Grand Lodge. A Master Mason is said to be Regular if he is a member in good standing, not suspended or expelled from his lodge. The Constitution consists of those laws according to which Masons act when they set up (erect or constitute) a lodge or a Grand Lodge. Once they are constituted, it is the body of laws under which lodges and Grand Lodges are governed in so far as "governed" means for them to continue to exist. A lodge's rules for its self-regulation are called *By-Laws*. A book containing the laws of the Grand Lodge is usually called its *Code*. There are many kinds of Masonic laws, Landmarks, Constitutions, Statutes, General Laws, Edicts, Decisions, Rules, Regulations, Customs, and Usages.

If a number of men, on their own, form a society, write its laws and ceremonies to suit their own purposes, and then call it (or miscall it) a "Masonic lodge," it is said to be *spurious*. It is said to be clandestine if it is, in work and ceremony, similar to a Masonic lodge but not on the List of a Grand Lodge. If a lodge is defective in its laws or practices, it is called *irregular;* when a Grand Lodge remedies these defects, it is said to be *healed*. When a Candidate gives his promises to obey the laws, rules, and regulations, it is called his *Obligation*, a word meaning "to tie together." His Oath or Vow is the part of his Obligation in which he pledges himself and submits himself to Masonic discipline.

If a member commits offenses as defined in the Grand Lodge's Code, the unruly member may be ordered to stand trial. The penalty may be suspension, expulsion, or other punishment if found guilty. The scope of a lodge's authority over Masonic discipline is called its *Penal Jurisdiction*. The word *Penalties* is also used for passages in the ritual that have been symbolic throughout the whole of Masonic history. The rules of order according to which a lodge conforms to civil and Masonic law requirements when operating as a body are called *Parliamentary Law*.

Such rules as having order, decorum, and correct behavior as their purpose are called *Etiquette*.

The word *ancient* is used in Freemasonry to mean "very old" or "time immemorial." The period from about 800 A. D. to the Reformation in the 16th Century is called by historians *The Middle Ages; Medieval* is the adjective describing that period. Therefore, Masonic historians say that our Fraternity had a Medieval origin. If today's Mason only realizes it, he steps into the Middle Ages when he steps into his lodge because in its nomenclature, form of organization, and rules and regulations, it has remained unchanged from Medieval times.

The words *Mason* and *Freemason* are themselves Medieval words. By *Operative* is meant a builder who practiced Masonry, that is, building and architecture, as a means of livelihood. *Speculative* is a Medieval word that means that the work is done by the mind rather than by the hands – geometry, designing, etc. *Symbolic Masonry* means the use of the ancient Craft for non-Operative purposes. *Transition* is the name of the period when non-Operative Petitioners began to be admitted, or accepted, into the lodges in great and increasing numbers. The *Operative Period* was that in which its membership was wholly Operative. It lasted from the end of the Dark Ages to about 1350. The *Transition Period* ran from about 1350 to about 1717. The *Speculative Period* (also called *Modern*) lasted from about 1717 to the present.

At the end of the 18th Century, new Masonic Bodies were organized around degrees additional to the Three Degrees. Those together are sometimes known as *The High Grades* and others being called variously "Concordant Orders," "Appendant Orders," "Further Degrees," etc. In the beginning, Ancient Craft Masonry included only the first Three Degrees but then became the foundation for other degrees. Capitular Freemasonry comprises the Royal Arch Degrees; Cryptic Freemasonry comprises the Cryptic

Degrees; Knight Templarism comprises the Templar Degrees; together they comprise the *American Rite* or more commonly, the *York Rite. Scottish Rite Freemasonry* covers all Scottish Rite Degrees, 1st to 33rd. Each of these separate sets of degrees is called a *Rite*. A Masonic Rite begins in its own unique craft degrees. "Blue Lodge" is Masonic slang and refers to the craft lodge. Masonry and Freemasonry are used interchangeably for convenience. Still, in the Operative Period, *Masonry* was the name for the whole Craft of builders, whereas Freemasons comprised only one branch. All Freemasons were Masons but not all Masons were Freemasons.

There are in Masonic nomenclature a number of terms and phrases not found elsewhere, which are in some instances rare and in a few instances are a puzzle to etymologists. *Due Guard* is such a puzzle; it may have come from the Old French. If so, it meant, "May God guard you." *Cowan* is believed to be an old Scottish name for any workman not in a guild – what in present-day trade union slang is called a "scab." The word in the Esoteric Work, which usually is pronounced "hail" but is spelled *hele*, is an old Anglo-Saxon term which meant "to hide by burying." An *oblong square* would be a self-contradiction in mathematics. It is an old colloquial name for a rectangle. The word *heal* means "to make whole." *Inchoate* is defined as meaning "not yet complete." A *tracing board* is a board on which Masons draw plans. *Recognition* does not mean only "to identify, to know" but includes "official approbation."

A *Masonic Glossary* lists the names and terms used in Freemasonry. A *Masonic Dictionary* consists exclusively of words used in the Fraternity. A *Masonic Encyclopedia* is like any other encyclopedia except that its subjects and articles are confined to Freemasonry. Freemasonry has no language (as the Roman Catholic Church has a Latin of its own) but uses the language of the people among whom its lodges are at work. Its nomenclature consists of the names and words used in it, emphasizing that in the Fraternity, they have definitions or usages peculiarly Masonic. A Mason's vocabulary are those names and words in the nomenclature he knows and uses among the many requirements for efficiency in lodge office. An ample Masonic vocabulary is most important.

The English language, as used in the Ritual of the Three Degrees in English-speaking lodges, is of great beauty. Much of it is very old. Among them are phrases white with age. Over it is that shrouding that no words and phrases can have until they have been used for generations. It is golden and eloquent and often rises to the levels of the highest poetry. To come into possession of such a vocabulary so that it becomes a part of his mind and passes into his own daily use is one of the rewards a present-day Masonic workman receives for his labors. This is so true that despite the secrecy of the lodge, a number of words and phrases have escaped it and entered into the people's daily speech. The word Freemasonry itself has become a common noun. "Meet on the level," "to act on the square," a "square deal," "who comes here," and "the Grand Architect" are familiar phrases everywhere. There are others not so obvious but equally numerous, and a man who is equally well-read in Freemasonry and general literature often encounters in poetry, essays, dramas, or novels-phrases, words and expressions, and intimations which he recognizes to be echoes out of the great and noble language of the Craft.

Chapter III
Transition

(Operative to Speculative Masonry)

For half of the eight centuries or more of its existence, Freemasonry consisted of craftsmen who worked for daily wages in one of the branches of architecture. Since they were workmen giving their full time to building in its literal and material sense, they were called *Operatives*. The centuries in which the Fraternity consisted wholly of them is called the *Operative Period.* Since the first quarter of the 18th Century, the same Fraternity has been composed wholly of non-Operatives. These are called *Speculative Masons*. The period between two and three centuries since the Craft passed into their hands is called the *Speculative Period.* The great and central problem for Masonic historians is to solve how the *Operative Fraternity* was transformed into the *Speculative Fraternity.*

The almost complete lack of written records left behind by the Operative Masons has made the problem an exceptionally difficult one to solve, yet historical scholars almost unanimously agreed that the crossing from the Operative Period to the Speculative Period was a slow one and carried on step by step, without planning, without conscious purpose, and that therefore it lasted over, at least, more than two centuries. That long stretch of time is called the *Transition Period.* Therefore, Freemasonry's history arranges itself under three general heads or into three large periods: The Operative, The Transitional, and The Speculative.

Masonic historians agreed on this arrangement as early as the latter half of the 1700s, but from then until about the early 1900s, they were not in agreement as to what it was which had occurred in The Transition Period. Their disagreement was so vast that a number of them gave up the hope of explaining how Operative Freemasonry could turn itself into something so unlike itself as Speculative Freemasonry. A number of them abandoned the belief that the Speculative Fraternity had ever derived from the Operative Fraternity and began to seek its origin elsewhere. During the 1900s, and thanks partly to an increase in the efficiency of Masonic research and partly to an increasingly successful hunt for written records, light is being seen. Masonic scholars have been reaching an agreement on the position that the Operative Fraternity was preserved and perpetuated in all its essentials except for literal building work. And that Speculative Freemasonry consisted of putting that ancient Fraternity to new use. The question of why they did so, and how they did so, is the subject matter of this history of the Transition Period.

If a history includes involves problems that are too difficult, complex, or numerous to be understandable to a non-historian, the writer has no choice but to over-simplify. Of course, to omit essential parts, make a problem appear easier than it is, and over-simplify are crimes against truth that no honorable historian can tolerate. Yet what would the non-historians desire or need to read history? What then can historians do? Thus far, no historian has found a way out of this dilemma except to go ahead and oversimplify and then make a full and candid confession that he has done so. And after he has thus absolved himself, he can address to his non-historian readers that ancient and wise adage, "We must do our best with what we have." It is one of the few instances in which *Caveat Emptor* ("let the buyer beware") becomes somewhat understandable.

The author must make such a confession of this book because its subject matter involves not only the nearly insoluble problem of the Transition Period but almost every other difficult Masonic problem. The quintessential substance of the book can be stated in a few sentences: Our Fraternity began as a Fraternity of Operative Freemasons at work in Britain and Europe long ago. But the particular Fraternity from which ours has descended (with no break in continuity) began with the Fraternity of those Operative Freemasons who discovered and perpetuated the Gothic style of architecture. Since the first known Gothic building was erected in Paris in 1140-1150, that is our earliest date. The real movement leading to Speculative Freemasonry was the forming of permanent and chartered lodges in about 1450. Non-Operative petitioners sought membership in those lodges because they found in them a number of truths not to be found elsewhere. These were truths about the subject of work, and these non-Operatives, once they were in control of the ancient Fraternity, put it to the new use of preserving and teaching those truths to men of any and all crafts, arts, trades, or professions. Our Speculative Fraternity is a continuation of that use. This is an oversimplification, but it is not a falsification. The argument on which it rests is such that if any Mason reads through and thinks through the whole body of our records and literature, he will arrive at the same conclusion.

Non-Operatives were accepted into the permanent, chartered lodges one at a time. There was never a planned or concerted movement of them. It is doubtful if any lodge became wholly Speculative (or "Accepted") before *about* 1600. But the explanation of the Transition from an Operative to a Speculative Fraternity does not lie in the increasing number of those accepted, non-Operatives, because the Operative membership could have stopped accepting them any time it wished. Instead, the secret lies in the new use which these accepted non-Operatives made of Operative Freemasonry. Since the Operative Masons themselves did not close the door on accepted non-Operatives (except in lodges here and there), it follows that the Operative Masons themselves approved of the new use to which their Fraternity was being put. A number of lodges refused to have themselves put to that new use. Many continued to use Freemasonry for Operative and Speculative purposes at the same time, but that is neither here nor there. That which carried Freemasonry through the Transition Period was the fact that finally so many lodges were wholly devoted to the new use that they were by 1717 able to erect a Grand Lodge System and made Freemasonry wholly Speculative. Operative Masonry in the sense of architecture and building activities continued as before, through the Transition and until now. In England, these builders organized a Fraternity of their own no fewer than three times, and they have one now. But these societies of practicing (or Operative) Masons lie outside the Speculative Fraternity, have no place in it, and have not had any say since about 1650.

In his *Concise History of Freemasonry*, published in 1903, Robert Freke Gould accounted for the Transition on the theory that the practice of accepting non-Operatives of itself, and without help from other facts or practices, led to the setting up of a Fraternity wholly Speculative. As instances of such acceptances, he gave a small list of members who left some record of their initiation behind them. Almost every other historian has repeated his list since. In it were such instances as Boswell, the Laird of Auchinleck, was accepted into the lodge of Edinburgh in 1600. The City Company of Masons in London had a division, possibly a side order, called "The Accepcion" at least as early as 1620. Elias Ashmole was made a Mason in a wholly Speculative Lodge at Warrington in 1646. Dr. Robert Plot referred to Freemasons in a book he published in 1686. Randle Holme described himself as a Freemason in a book he published in 1688. A lodge at Aberdeen prepared what it called *The Lodge Book* in 1670 and proved itself to be part Operative, part Speculative, and to have an outdoor ceremony (which sounds like our Third Degree).

There was a Speculative Lodge at York in 1705. *The Book of Constitutions*, published in 1723, referred to lodges and Christopher Wren as Grand Master following the London fire in 1666. So far as the individuals mentioned are concerned, they mean nothing because doubtless some non-Operative members had been accepted into Operative Lodges, temporary or permanent, from the first. The principal value of such a catalog of instances lies in its proof that there were Speculative Lodges at least as early as 1646. The oldest version of the *Old Charges* speaks of non-Operatives as having been in the Craft in ancient times and does so without further comment.

Gould's theory was that at about 1600, a few non-Operatives were accepted into membership. While the number was few at first, it slowly increased; and Speculative Freemasonry resulted when the number of Accepted Masons (or Speculatives – the terms are here used interchangeably) overtook the number of Operative members. A theory of simple arithmetical increase would thus explain the problem of the Transition. But this is only to state the problem and does not solve it. Why did the number of Accepted Masons increase? William James Hughan had a theory of another kind, namely, that Speculative Freemasonry, of itself, "grew out of," or developed out of, Operative Freemasonry, and therefore his explanation of the Transition means that the Transition represented nothing but the mere passage of time. But this leaves too much unexplained. Why didn't Speculative "grow out of" Operative centuries before? It had plenty of time. Why did it grow out of it in England only when Operative Freemasonry had been the same on the Continent as there? When the first lodges, either half Speculative or wholly Speculative, were formed, there was a vast amount of Operative Masonry outside those lodges; why didn't it develop into Speculative Freemasonry? There is an even larger amount of Operative building now, organized in hundreds of unions. Is there any trace, at all, of Speculative Freemasonry in the process of formation in these unions? If the whole body of Operative Freemasonry in Britain grew into Speculative Freemasonry, why is it that the history of our Fraternity invariably leads back to a (comparatively) few and small permanent lodges using copies of the Old Charges? Neither the idea of growth nor of inevitable development can explain the Transition. Something special was at work. Something new arose. Speculative Freemasonry did not come out of Operative Freemasonry in general, but out of that, something new and something unique. What that was has been already explained. In a few early permanent lodges, their members began to put Freemasonry to new use, and whether this was done by the Operative members first or the Speculative members first does not matter; they both approved it, and they joined together in doing it.

If historians had sufficiently pictorial eyes, they could lay out the whole two-and-one-half centuries in the form of a panoramic picture. As this was unrolled from the top, it would show the following in one chronological portion of the picture after another: There had always been much of what we now call Speculative in the earliest Operative Craft. We inherited not only the ideas, customs, and usages of the lodges and the Craftsmen at work but the essentials of the whole Masonic Community. Our particular Speculative Fraternity came to us through the lodges, which became permanent, and used the Old Charges beginning at about the middle of the 14th Century. Accepted Masons took the same oath to preserve the secrets and not to violate the Landmarks as did Operative members. Their historic mission was not to destroy an old Fraternity in order to put a new one in its place (why go to that trouble?) but to preserve and perpetuate the old Fraternity and yet, at the same time to put it to a new use. The subsequent history of what they did proves that that new use was of very great and very vital importance to the world. There were hundreds of self-constituted lodges in England, Scotland, and Ireland before 1717, some of them wholly Operative, some wholly Speculative, some a mixture of both. When a few of these constituted a Grand Lodge in London in 1717, it did not disturb the local lodges already at work. It was not until the new Grand Lodge System proved so extraordinarily effective over the period about 1750 that the whole Fraternity became completely Speculative. It would be a mistake to suppose that this Transition was carried through by the Accepted (or non-Operative, or Speculative) members and lodges only and as against Operative opposition. Operative Lodges could always refuse to accept a non-Operative petitioner and would have done so had they been in opposition. The Accepted Masons may have seen Freemasonry's possible universality and world importance more clearly than the Operatives. Nevertheless, the Fraternity (speaking of the whole) was brought through the Transition by Operatives and Speculatives combined.

Superficially akin to Gould's theory that the Transition was accomplished by adding members and to Hughan's theory of inevitable growth was the once widely held theory that Speculative Freemasonry grew from Operative because tradition has always had a powerful appeal to Englishmen. The Operative Masons, as the argument explains, kept up a set of customs and usages for many generations. After these customs and usages had ceased to have any value to Operative Masons, non-Operatives continued to keep them going because they did not have the heart to see anything so venerable or so beautiful (like old ivory) brought to an end. According to this theory, the Transition consisted of nothing more than the willingness of a large number of non-Operatives to keep alive a set of customs after the men to whom those customs had belonged were no longer willing to continue them. This theory had almost everything wrong with it that could be wrong with a theory. Speculative Freemasonry began long before Operative Masons had ceased to keep up their usages and customs. Speculative Freemasonry has old customs and usages but does not consist of them. It is possible to believe that a few Englishmen would rather continue old customs than see them die, but the number of Masons in England has never been few. The theory cannot explain why some millions of Americans would be willing to keep up a set of old English customs during and after the Revolutionary War Period when our National Fraternity was established. Americans were not enamored of old English customs!

The theory never had anything more than guesswork and of an amateurish kind. But it was no more completely a piece of guesswork than a companion theory that once was in vogue in the United States. This theory was that Operative Freemasonry died, came to a dead stop, fell into ruins, and that a number of gentlemen of the club mind set up in London a new Fraternity for which, for the sake of making it more venerable in appearance, and to give it a cachet of mystery or secrecy, they borrowed the trappings of defunct Freemasonry. If this theory were true, historians would drop the Transition Period from the books because there could have been no Transition. There was a dead stop for and of Operative Freemasonry, a short gap, and a wholly new society was organized among the ruins. Of the many facts that stand ready to refute this amazing notion, this will suffice – it completely ignores the many Speculative Lodges at work a century before 1717. It ignores the Speculative elements which were always in Operative Freemasonry, it ignores the fact that Operatives as much as Speculatives built up the Speculative Fraternity, and it ignores the fact that the new Grand Lodge of 1717 was not created out of hand but was an action taken (even during its first two or three years) by at least twenty lodges which were in existence before 1717.

CHAPTER IV
THE FIRST GRAND LODGE

In Britain in the Middle Ages, Operative Freemasonry was the name for the art of architecture. This art consisted of a fixed body of knowledge that each apprentice had to learn, and much of it by heart. Once he had learned, his own Freemasonry was the same as every other Freemason. During the long period in which there were no permanent lodges, Grand Lodges, Books of Constitutions, or written laws, it was their possession of this one body of knowledge that gave unity of purpose to thousands of men who lived and worked here and there and had no general or national organization.

Freemasonry was self-constitutive. If a Master Mason was in need of an Apprentice, and if a qualified youth was available, he and a small number of other Master Masons could constitute themselves a lodge, enter him, give him his oath, and sign his indenture – to do this, they had no need to ask consent from any Masonic body. The same Master Masons, if called to work together, could constitute themselves as a lodge, select their officers, and meet as a lodge as long as the work lasted. If Master Masons in a country, city, or other convenient area, whether in any lodge at the time or not, found it necessary to confer among themselves on Craft matters, they could meet in a self-constituted assembly. In the 14th Century, the Freemasons in a few centers began to organize permanent lodges under written charters. Those lodges were also self-constituted. Nothing in the Craft was more Masonic, or more truly a landmark, than this inherent right to constitute assemblies or bodies when there was the need. Even the Masonic Companies in large cities, which lasted for so many centuries and functioned in one way or another as a part of the municipal government, were self-constitutive.

Acting on this time-immemorial right and believing that the Craft would benefit by having a permanent General Assembly, a small number of representatives from several of the oldest London lodges (we have the names of four) met in 1716 in the Apple Tree Tavern. They agreed (though acting for their lodges) "to cement under a Grand Master as the center of Union and Harmony." On St. John the Baptist's Day in 1717, the same representatives met at the Goose and Gridiron Ale-house (one of the four lodges met in its room) and "constituted themselves a Grand Lodge *pro Tempore* in Due Form" and "resolved to hold the Annual Assembly and Feast, and to choose a Grand Master from among themselves, till they should have the Honour of a Noble Brother at their Head." Mr. Anthony Sayer, Gentleman, was elected Grand Master; Jacob Lambdall, a carpenter, and Captain Joseph Elliot, were elected Grand Wardens. This desire to have a "Noble Brother" at their head was not an act of snobbery but followed a general rule in the nation that called for each society or large organization to have a sponsor from the ruling class who could act as spokesman in high places. The King himself consented to sponsor a society of scientists, so it called itself the Royal Society. A hundred years later, Freemasonry itself was to have a royal sponsor when Queen Victoria named herself to that honor.

The history of constituting the first, or Mother Grand Lodge, as given in the 1738 (second) Edition of the *Book of Constitutions*, is brief and of bare simplicity. But from the wealth of knowledge about it which we have from other sources, as well as from history following its founding, we know that it opened a new era in Freemasonry. The dawn of the Operative Craft, constituting a system of permanent lodges with the Old Charges in the 14th Century, and the erection of the Mother Grand Lodge are the epochal events according to which our Craft dates the calendars of its history. The facts about the Mother Grand Lodge as we know them prove a number of things:

1. There were lodges at work before 1717. Some of them were composed of Operative Freemasons, some were composed partly of Operatives and partly of Speculative Freemasons, and some were wholly composed of Speculative members.

2. General Assemblies (with Feasts) existed before 1717; the new Grand Lodge became a Permanent assembly with continuous functions. Why a permanent Assembly? Partly because it had become too inconvenient to call special assemblies, partly because the lodges had come to need a "center of union" continually.

3. Constituting a permanent Grand Lodge for the first time was not an innovation. The older Masons and lodges resented a few new measures taken after the Grand Lodge had been at work for five or ten years, but they did not oppose a Grand Lodge in the first place because they saw in it only a new way of doing something which had been done in other ways for centuries.

4. To constitute the new Grand Lodge, the representatives of the old lodges employed the old methods for constituting a lodge, therefore there was no innovation and nothing radical. The Grand Lodge was to be a lodge, and it would differ from other lodges only in having lodges for its members instead of individual Masons. The *Book of Constitutions* itself, first published in 1723, was, in theory and fact, nothing but the Old Charges revised to suit the needs of a Grand Lodge.

5. The new Grand Lodge did not attempt to change, modify, or alter the Work used in the lodges. By the principle of its constitution as well as by common consent, it left to each member lodge its own old local sovereignty. Each lodge retained unimpaired its own Landmarks, its own Officers, conferred its own degrees, examined, and

made its own Candidates, and continued to be supreme within its own local jurisdiction. (A minute analysis of the records and Minute Books of six lodges that had existed before 1717 A.D., and which afterward became member lodges as it did not show that any of them altered its Work after going on the Grand Lodge list.) This fact holds true even to this day, more than two centuries after 1717 A.D., although the increased number of lodges and Grand Lodges make it more difficult to see, a lodge is still sovereign in its own local jurisdiction, the Grand Lodge is sovereign over only such matters and questions as rise among the lodges.

6. The first Grand Lodge claimed jurisdiction only over lodges on its own List, and in the beginning, these lodges were to be confined to London and Westminster. Any number of other Grand Lodges could have been constituted at the time without conflicting with it. It was not until years later that it began to put on its list lodges outside of London, and it was not until 1813 A.D. that a Grand Lodge had the whole of England for its jurisdiction. Even then, its jurisdiction did not extend over Scotland or Ireland. Also, it delegated a certain amount of its authority to a number of Provincial Grand Lodges of its own.

7. The founding of the first Grand Lodge proved, in the long run, not to have been the founding of a simple Grand Body in London, but the establishing of the Grand Lodge System. That system has become essential to Freemasonry. It has molded so much of Freemasonry about itself that it is a Landmark, and it would be now unthinkable to tear it up by the roots because to do so would destroy the Fraternity.

8. These facts, and others like them, are interesting, and each is highly important. But none of them rank in importance with the fact that the establishment of the Grand Lodge System was epoch-making in the complete and literal sense of that adjective. This is the fact that with

the Grand Lodge System, the Fraternity became wholly, once and for all, a Speculative Fraternity. Yes, there had been Speculative Lodges before 1717. There had always been a sizeable Speculative element in Operative Freemasonry. But either the complete or partial control of the Fraternity had been in the hands of the Operatives until it passed, with the coming of the Grand Lodge System, wholly into the hands of Speculatives.

9. When the Grand Lodge of 1717 is called *The Mother Grand Lodge*, it does not mean that it constituted other Grand Lodges or "mothered" them after they were constituted. The Grand Lodges in Scotland, Ireland, at York, and the Ancient Grand Lodge, constituted in London in 1751, were self-constituted. They neither asked nor received authorization from the first Grand Lodge. That continues to be the rule because where there are three or four regular lodges anywhere in the world that work in an area or territory where no other regular Grand Lodge exists, they can constitute a Grand Lodge. It will receive recognition from other Grand Lodges if it is regularly constituted. There is no special significance in the fact that the first Grand Lodge was erected in London instead of in some other city. It could have been constituted in 1700 or 1730, as well as in 1717. The old lodges which formed it were not unique but practiced the same Masonry as old lodges anywhere in England, Scotland, or Ireland. Nevertheless, the glory which belongs to men who do something for the first time will always be attached to it. It was fortunate for the Fraternity when it had its first permanent General Assembly at last that its headquarters should be in London, the nation's capital. It stood close to the center of the British Empire and from which the new Grand Lodge System could make its way more easily and rapidly than from any other source.

From 1717 until about 1735, the new Grand Lodge went on slowly and cautiously, completing itself in which, with extraordinary good fortune, it used such leaders as Desaguliers, Anderson, and Payne. It warranted lodges abroad and set up Provincial Grand Lodges in America. Its relations with the short-lived Grand Lodge at York were amicable, and it was in close cooperation with the Grand Lodges in Scotland and Ireland. There was no cloud in the sky. And then, about 1735, and as historiographers say, it began to enter a new cultural "climate." Though its members had no more knowledge than other men, certain small events and new social changes were the beginnings of what by 1775 was to become a world-revolutionary change, not in England only but everywhere. During that world-revolutionary change, Masonry itself was to become no longer a British, or even European, Fraternity but a worldwide Fraternity. This fundamental shift occurred in the Grand Lodge during a somewhat strange and puzzling chapter in its history which it called "Modern." That chapter lasted for about forty years (with emphasis on the "about"). When Masonic historians and other writers refer to "Modern Masonry" or "The Modern Grand Lodge," they are referring to that chapter. This has to be because before about 1735, the Grand Lodge was not yet "Modern," and after about 1775, it had ceased to be "Modern." It is impossible to compress a detailed history of that period into one or two pages, but it can be characterized as:

1. In 1723, the Grand Lodge had the opportunity to "choose a Noble Brother" for its head when the Duke of Montague consented to become Grand Master. He was followed by the Duke of Wharton, and from then on, the Grand East was occupied by a man of very high title. As things then were in British society, this set up a chain of consequences that the Grand Lodge itself was helpless to avoid, for the prerogatives of rank were inviolable. A "Noble" Grand Master would look for social equals to fill other Grand Lodge Offices. He selected them to be Provincial Grand Masters, and in due course, local lodges

began to seek their Officers in the aristocracy. According to the laws and rules of rank, a man of high rank could never set aside the authorities, privileges, and prerogatives of his rank. Therefore, if a Duke sat in the Grand East, he sat there primarily as a Duke and only secondarily (and almost only in a token capacity) as Grand Master. This imported the whole system of British aristocracy into the Fraternity and, in so doing, opened an unbridged chasm between Masons of the "upper classes" and Masons of the "lower classes." This was an innovation because the equality of Masons, and the right of any Mason to hold an Office, had been a Landmark since the earliest days.

2. In a time when there were no daily newspapers, telephones, movies, etc., the feelings of the London public found an outlet in the theater, in coffee house gossip, pamphlets, caricatures, and popular songs. Since it was a period of general vulgarity, those feelings were more likely than not to be sarcastic or satirical. Once the new Grand Lodge had come to the attention of "the town," it became a target for mock processions, parodies, satires, ridicule, and ironic skits in the theater. In the midst of this, and thanks to the mania for pamphleteering, a number of pamphlets and broadsides were published which purported to "expose" the "secrets" of the Craft. To protect itself against these irritations, the Grand Lodge resorted to expedients that were more drastic than wise; it forbade public processions, censored Masonic speeches and publications, made alterations in the Modes of Recognition, permitted an emasculation of the ritual, and permitted the ceremonies of Installation of lodge Officers to lapse.

3. Many lodges resented the innovations in the Modes of Recognition not because the particular form of those Modes was of significant importance but because changing of the ritual involved a reversal of a principle as old as the Craft. The ritual was sacrosanct; a Master Mason could not

alter it, a lodge could not, a Grand Lodge could not, and each Grand Lodge Officer had taken an oath not to violate the Landmarks in the ritual. Therefore, when the Grand Lodge so acted as to set itself above the ritual it was guilty of an innovation, and lodges rebelled against the innovation.

4. The Grand Lodge permitted the use of the *Ceremonies of Installation* to be abandoned. Again, the Ceremonies themselves were not crucial, but the principle involved was important. The point of those Ceremonies was that an authority was inherent in Lodge Offices and that no Grand Master or Grand Lodge could override that inherent authority. When it dropped these Ceremonies, the Grand Lodge did, in fact, override it. The real meaning of dropping the Ceremonies was, in effect, to reduce the Mastership to a position of no genuine authority. This meant that lodges could not be self-constituted or self-governing and that lodges everywhere would be governed from the headquarters of the Grand Lodge. A Grand Master would rule and govern lodges as well as the Grand Lodge.

5. The "emasculation of the ritual," which meant cutting its content to a minimum and consequent lowering of its dignity, was itself disheartening. But its damage was only a symptom of a greater trouble. As more and more "gentlemen" came into the lodges, as Masonic offices more and more were filled with members of the aristocracy, many of the lodges ceased to be *Masonic* lodges and became social clubs. "Masonic Purpose" were no longer to make Masons but to have nights of conviviality. The full ritual took up too much time; it got in the road of conviviality; the emasculation, therefore, resulted in turning lodges of Freemasonry into places of social enjoyment.

The whole process, characterized by these five explanations, was gradual; neither the Grand Lodge itself nor any of its lodges intended to undermine the foundations of the Fraternity by malice. Their intentions, such as they had, were completely innocent in their own eyes. A well-informed historian is willing to write off the unfortunate consequences of their "Modernizing" the Craft (it was their own word) to the fact that the Speculative Fraternity (as Speculative) was still in its youth. Many of its members did not understand the Landmarks or know anything of Masonic history. They were unfamiliar with ancient rules, regulations, customs, and laws.

During the period in which these conditions were obtained, the Grand Lodge, which had begun in 1717, was called "the Modern Grand Lodge." It was called by that name because it chose it for itself to emphasize its having "modernized" the ancient Fraternity. But when after a period of some forty years (a little over one generation), it began to see how the consequences necessarily implied in its "modernization" were working out, and it learned at a somewhat bitter cost what the consequences were (the Grand Lodges of Ireland and Scotland had withdrawn recognition from it). The Grand Lodge desisted from a course that it had found to be filled with innovation and returned by its own actions to the Ancient Landmarks. After doing so, Masons continued to call it the Modern Grand Lodge but only to distinguish it from the other Grand Lodge of England; in reality, it had ceased to be "Modern."

It is, therefore, not historically correct to apply the name "Modern" to the *Mother Grand Lodge*, which worked uninterruptedly from 1717 to the *Union of 1813*, because the word characterizes only one chapter in a long history. While that which it characterizes was a mistake on the part of the Grand Lodge, it was not a fatal error. In due time it was rectified. Its leaders in the latter half of the 18th Century were to be clearly seen as leaders. It was not the destiny of the Ancient Craft to be transfigured into a system of British Clubs. Its honor and the tale of its achievements stand out above any other Grand Lodge in the world. It was the first. It built its foundations so securely and erected upon them its own super-structure so skillfully that succeeding Grand Lodges had only to use the blueprints it had drawn and publish over again the *Book of Constitutions* which it had written. Under it, the *Standard Monitor* was first prepared and published. It was the Mother of Lodges beyond the seas, the model for Grand Lodges in lands of which Payne and Anderson had never heard. It planted Freemasonry in the Americas, where it was to have a century later a growth that out-topped the Craft's previous history. It established the Grand Lodge System. By the wisdom of its early statesmanship, it found a way to turn the whole Fraternity around on its pivot from Operative to Speculative without undoing the long work of the past. At one point or another, to some degree or other, each and every regular lodge in the world can trace something of its origin back to the Goose and Gridiron Ale-house on that day in 1717, when some thirty or so brethren decided to erect "a Grand Lodge *pro Tempore* in Due Form."

CHAPTER V
"ANCIENT" MASONRY

In and about the year 1740, Ireland belonged as much to Great Britain as England did, or Scotland. English families lived in Ireland, Irish families lived in England, and Ireland had its share of peers in the House of Lords as later it was to have its share of members in the House of Commons. So was it with Freemasonry. The Grand Lodge of Ireland was recognized by it. More than one was a member of lodges in Ireland and lodges in England at the same time. There was freedom to visit and freedom to demit. If a member of a regular Irish lodge lived in London, he was as much of a Mason in the eyes of his brothers there as any member in a London lodge.

In the 1740s, Ireland suffered from a series of potato famines which for more than a century were as much a curse to the country as any disastrous war. It was the Irish peasant who had suffered most tragically. Men and women starved to death in the towns and cities, and many fled to other countries. Many professional men, skilled workmen, and tradesmen moved to London because they had relatives or friends there. Among these emigrants, a sizable number were members of Irish lodges.

According to the Ancient Landmarks, rules, and regulations, these Irish brothers had the same rights to visit and to demit as London Masons. Nevertheless, when they sought to do so, they were turned back at the door. The reason that they were turned back was made abundantly clear to them when they were told that too many of them were carpenters, plumbers, stonemasons, teamsters, and similar members of the "lower classes." The London lodges' officers, aristocrats, and gentlemen of fastidious taste, refused to foregather in the Lodge Room or to sit at a table with anybody from the "lower classes." These gentlemen wore a workingman's leather apron; they had accepted working tools when they took their obligations; they were officers in a Craft founded and exclusively manned by workingmen for centuries. But even their own noses, sharpened by the insolence of their class, could detect no self-contradiction in their refusing to sit with Masons in a Masonic lodge if a Mason was a carpenter. Jesus of Nazareth could not have visited such a lodge. This snobbishness was an extraordinary and fateful result of the "modernizing" of the Fraternity, which was underway, and of which boasting was being made.

After it became apparent that this exclusiveness had become a rule, and not a temporary aberration, a number of these Irish Masons, with the assistance and approval of the Grand Lodge of Ireland, constituted a few lodges of their own. They had an inherent and constitutional right to do so, and it could be done without violating the Jurisdiction of the Grand Lodge in London. The unfortunate law of *Exclusive Territorial Jurisdiction* not yet having been enacted. During this same period, a number of lodges on the list of the Grand Lodge at London (which had been constituted in 1717 by four old lodges of which only one had a membership of "gentlemen") became so resentful at this new exclusiveness, and so violently disapproved of the innovations of which the Grand Lodge had become guilty, that they began to withdraw from it. By the end of the decade of 1740-1750, when one Irish Mason withdrew himself from the Grand Lodge at London, ten English Masons had done so.

Along with them, and agreeing with them, were a hundred or so independent regular lodges (called St. John's Lodges), which had never been on the Grand Lodge's Lists. This refusal to recognize the so-called "modernizing" of Freemasonry reached such a pitch at the last that the Grand Lodges of Ireland and Scotland withdrew recognition from the Grand Lodge at London. It was called "Grand Lodge at London" because England was not a single Grand Jurisdiction at the time and was not to become one until 1813. There was, in any real sense of the name, no Grand Lodge of England. When the *Grand Lodge of All England at York* gave itself that title, it only meant it was willing to receive into its membership lodges from any part of England.

After they had set up two or three lodges, each of which was regular and duly constituted and so recognized by the Grand Lodges of Ireland and Scotland, they formed a Grand Committee as a center of union. This Committee was made into a Grand Lodge by the usual regular and duly constituted method in 1751. To show that it had repudiated the "modernizing" of Masonry and would never approve or accept it in the future, it gave itself the title of a Grand Lodge "according to the Ancient Institutions." For that reason, it came to be called "The Ancient" Grand Lodge, not in slang or derision, but seriously and respectfully. The Ancient Grand Lodge was a single Grand Lodge with headquarters in London and had no jurisdiction over anything except the lodges on its list.

Under normal circumstances, one Grand Lodge would have been but one among many. The Ancient Grand Lodge would not have loomed up in the Craft at large until, at one time, it almost filled the horizon. Its name would never have been used to describe a great new stage in the development of the Fraternity, a development without which we could never have had a worldwide Fraternity. It would not now stand in our history alongside the Grand Lodge of 1717 and with an importance second only to that Mother Grand Body. But the circumstances were not normal in Freemasonry then, and as the events were to prove a half-century later. The Ancient Grand Lodge itself, along with the Modern Grand Lodge, was to be swept up and enveloped and carried along by that universal groundswell to make the Fraternity universal as it always had been potentially and in principle.

The Grand Lodge of 1717 (which kept a separate existence until 1813) is not correctly called "The Modern Grand Lodge" except during the forty years or so in which it was guilty of the innovations of class distinctions, exclusiveness, alteration in the nature of Masonic offices, emasculation of the ritual, etc. If "Ancient Grand Lodge" means a Grand Lodge which waged open warfare on that "modernization," that name similarly can be correctly used by the Grand Lodge of 1751. For when the lodges under the older Grand Lodge had ceased to carry on chosen innovations, there was no difference between the Work done in the lodges under the one and the lodges under the other. At any time after 1790, the two could have merged as they were to do in 1813. Therefore, if by "Ancient" is meant that which was opposed to "Modern," the Grand Lodge of 1751 itself ceased to be "Ancient" after the Grand Lodge of 1717 had ceased to be "Modern."

At about the time of the American and the French Revolutions (1775-1795), Freemasonry entered that period of universality in which it now stands and the transition from a Fraternity primarily British and European into one genuinely worldwide. It had a center nowhere because its centers were everywhere. It opened a new era in our history, only slightly less epoch-making than the founding of the Grand Lodge System. The Ancient Grand Lodge did not by itself inaugurate or control the entrance of the Fraternity into its era as a worldwide Fraternity. Still, it contributed so much to that end that its contributions are its title to fame. (Newly-Made Masons will discover that the account of the Modern vs the Ancient Grand Lodges, which they will find in the Masonic histories written before 1900, is very different from the account given here. With only a few exceptions, the facts about the Ancient Grand Lodge were not discovered until about 1900, and even now, are not widely known or clearly understood and universally accepted.)

1. Although the Ancient Grand Lodge of 1751 had on its list only a few lodges, and they were Irish members, it lost this Irishism in a short time when scores of English lodges began to accept its jurisdiction. Except in its formative period, it was as English as the Grand Lodge of 1717.

2. It had the great good fortune to have as its Grand Secretary Brother Laurence Dermott from 1752 to 1771. R. F. Gould described him as a callous-handed house painter with little education. That was because almost nothing was known about Dermott when Gould wrote his history. Born in Dublin in 1720, Dermott became a Mason in 1740 and

served as Worshipful Master in 1746. Shortly after, he moved to London, where he was elected Grand Secretary of the New Grand Lodge at the early age of thirty-two. He died in 1791. Dermott was what Eighteenth Century men called a genius. It was a small class of great men of which Christopher Wren and William Shakespeare were more famous specimens. Dermott was an interior decorator in early life, but Freemasonry became his profession after 1753 (like our own Brothers A. G. Mackey and Albert Pike). He had many talents, and they were of high excellence. He was a learned man (he could read Ancient Hebrew), a forceful and even powerful writer, as is proved by the *Book of Constitutions*, which he wrote. He was a singer, an after-dinner speaker (men traveled many miles to hear him), an organizer, and an administrator. He was a driving, daring, bold, tireless, ingenious, and inventive character with an enormous and almost intuitive understanding of Freemasonry. Who were the greatest Masons of that century? Desaguliers? Preston? The Duke of Sussex? Thomas Smith Webb? If so, Dermott belongs to the list because he ranks second in achievement to none of these names.

3. The Ancient Grand Lodge used the *Modes of Recognition* and the *Ceremonies of Installation* according to ancient usage. Instead of emasculating the ritual, they did the opposite. They restored the Work to its full plentitude, permitting nothing to interfere with it. They emphasized its primary importance, enacting it instead of reducing it to lecture form, and officially approved using the Royal Arch Degree. With this doctrine of the importance of the ritual and each item of the ritual in its complete form, the Grand Lodges of Scotland and Ireland agreed, and most lodges in America afterward came into agreement. The emasculated, localistic, and very British version of the ritual used so half-heartedly in the "Modern" lodges would never have carried Freemasonry over the seas and around the world,

partly because it was too meager and partly because it was too British. A lodge could only use the "Modern" version half-heartedly because its ritual and its practices contradicted each other. A Newly-Made Mason should note that any question about the ritual is a question of what Freemasonry is or is not. If anything is true of the ritual, it is that one of the cornerstones is that Masons "meet upon the level." Another cornerstone is that any worthy Master Mason may hold office. In one form or another, directly or by implication, literally or symbolically, the ritual is a series of statements about what it is to be a Mason – it is how a lodge "makes" a Mason. To omit something from the ritual is to omit it from Freemasonry.

4. The Ancient Grand Lodge employed Ambulatory (or Travelling) Warrants for lodges. Ireland began their use of this at about the same time. The practice began as an expedient. It was useful during a period in which world Masonry was in the process of formation. But except in a few Grand jurisdictions, it is no longer permitted. While it lasted, it was an agency that played a large part in Masonic history. An Ambulatory Warrant usually was issued to a lodge composed of soldiers or sailors. It gave the lodge a name, a number, and a first address, but expressly permitted the lodge members to carry the Warrant with them and act under it at any place they might be stationed. Thus, a lodge might receive a Warrant while its soldier members were stationed in Ireland. The lodge might move to one or two stations in England, Canada, the American Colonies, and India. Many lodge histories show an itinerary of that type. The practice was continued in the United States for three-quarters of a century after the Revolutionary War. lodges in Texas, the Southwest, and the Far West worked under charters carried about in wagons or saddlebags. The practice explains why there were so many lodges in the armies on both sides in the Revolutionary War. It explains why lodges were set up in

so many remote parts in Asia at so early a date, and why Freemasonry was carried literally over the world in only one or two generations.

5. Fundamental in the Ancient Grand Lodge was the invincible determination that in each and every lodge everywhere it should be the first duty of the Craft to keep inviolate that Ancient Landmark which ordains that Masons "meet upon the level." Once a man has been Raised to the Sublime Degree of Master Mason, no Mason shall stand higher or lower in any scale than he does — an Earl of Moira or a Duke of Sussex might preside in its Grand East, but if so, he would preside there as a Mason, and not as duke or earl. There is a principle in any aristocracy and its corollaries of exclusiveness and snobbishness with which historians have not dealt as they should, which sincere apologists for aristocracy overlook, and which defenders of it try to evade. It is the principle that the amount of exclusiveness and snobbishness increases in the geometric ratio in proportion to the distance from the center (or base) of the aristocracy in question. If I take it that I belong, by right of heredity, to an upper class, where you to be a lower class, I shall look down on you and exclude you from my circle. I'll do this even though you are also a man and a fellow countryman. I shall increase that exclusiveness toward a man from the Colonies; then I shall increase it once again, double it perhaps, toward a man of the Yellow Race; and then quadruple it toward a man of the Black Race. If Freemasonry had not sincerely and wholeheartedly adopted the principle that any qualified man of any race or creed is eligible to petition and that each Master Mason stands on the level with every other one, it would have been confined to the British Isles or at least to English-speaking peoples. It could never have established itself in fifty or sixty countries among men of the three great Races

and fifty or sixty sub-Races. But has Freemasonry completely purged itself of all racism?

6. Finally, by officially endorsing and practicing the Royal Arch Degree and having Ireland and Scotland unite with it, the Ancient Grand Lodge established in the Craft the principle of the High Grades. Since it thus established it, the principle has never been questioned. The point calls loudly for attention, which it has never received. It also calls to be re-appraised by our Masonic historians because their absorption of the internal histories of the High Grades has thrown no light on the great importance of the High Grades in assisting to make it possible for ours to become a World Fraternity. The Ancient Craft Freemasonry embodied in the Three Degrees is undoubtedly Operative in origin. Operative in its bone and marrow, but it also is in its bone and marrow English Operative. It owed so little to Operative Freemasonry in Europe that after 1717, European countries had to import Speculative Freemasonry from England. Now the Ancient Craft Ritual has much to say; it has so much to say that it says everything, but it is in a form native to English-speaking peoples. It is the great function of the High Grades in World Masonry to say that same thing and then to go on to say it in another form — thus and to give only one example, it is a fact, provable by endless written records and statistics, that the idiom of Scottish Rite Freemasonry is peculiarly appealing and intelligible to men in Latin countries. The more than forty degrees of the whole system of the five Masonic Rites give Freemasonry an amplitude and flexibility of voice to make itself understandable to men in any of the world's cultures. Establishing the principles of the High Grades officially and permanently inside the Fraternity was not accomplished by the Ancient Grand Lodge but by a consensus of many lodges in many lands and helped to inaugurate the era of World Masonry. But the Ancient Grand Lodge first saw the true principle of

the High Grades, and it belonged to its historic mission to be the first Grand Lodge to act upon it.

The history of the Ancient Grand Lodge is thus composed of two histories. There is a history of it as a single Grand Body in London, born as it was through default in the Grand Lodge of 1717, in rivalry (most of it local) with that Grand Lodge, and conscious of having the mission to restore to the Craft in England certain ancient usages and customs. That history, so often cold, is colorful and sometimes dramatic. Still, in the whole sweep of the Craft's history or against the background of World Masonry, it dwindles into comparative insignificance. The other history is the story of the rise within the Ancient Grand Lodge, and almost coincidentally in the Grand Lodges of Ireland and Scotland, of the beginnings of, and preparations for, chat which was to become World Masonry. That movement was too large for any Grand Lodge; it drew the Grand Lodge of 1717 into itself (William Preston helped to bring this about) and, in time, drew every regular Grand Lodge into it.

CHAPTER VI
MASONRY AS AN ORDER

Many newly-made Masons are confused by hearing the Fraternity called by a half dozen other descriptive names. It is as if its own members had never yet decided in their minds whether it is, in reality, a Fraternity, a lodge, a Brotherhood, an Association, a Society, a Craft, an Order, a Rite, a Fellowship, a Guild, or an Art. And at one time, it might also have been called by the now obsolete or unfamiliar name of Mystery. What, exactly, is it? The only clear answer that can be given is that it is *Freemasonry,* which cannot be classified with anything else. It possesses properties or forms of many kinds of associations. So, when a Mason calls it a lodge and then a society, etc., etc., he is thinking about one aspect of it and at another time is thinking about another. Freemasonry is, in strict and literal fact, many kinds of associations, and is all of them at one time. It is multiform. A Mason is not compelled to choose one descriptive name out of many but may use any of them as best suits his needs.

The word *Order* has an air about it of something hard, something arbitrary. It is always connected in our minds with the days when a parent "ordered us about" at home, a teacher in school, a sergeant snapped out orders in the army, or a foreman yelled orders in the shop. It carries with it, in consequence, overtones of arbitrariness, authority, harshness, and the use of force. Also, it has an air of being undemocratic and is closely and necessarily connected with the idea of rank, or ranks. Order has in it these and a number of other related meanings. It is, as it stands, a Latin word, and it means that men or things are in an arrangement, that each thing is placed, that there is no confusion, and that everything is planned and ranked according to such categories as time, size, or function.

The word also is connected in our minds with certain types of organizations which have been called "Orders" for the past 1500 years, such as the Order of the Knights Templar, the Teutonic Order, the Benedictine Order, the Order of the Garter, the Order of Malta, the Order of the Hospital, and many others. These associations and organizations did not give the word its meaning. Except in Templarism, we Masons are careful not to permit the use of the word to define what we mean when we say that our Fraternity is an Order because it has very little in common with the rules and regulations of the Orders of Chivalry. In Ancient Craft Masonry, we use the word in its common and original sense, whereas the Orders use it uniquely. Those Orders, of which the Order of the Temple is the most familiar example, were established by some man, a Pope, an Abbot, a King, etc., and began with a set of rules drawn for the purpose and at that time. Freemasonry is an Order not because it was initiated to be such by any one man. Freemasonry gradually grew to be an Order and as a consequence of historical causes.

When a lodge of Operative Freemasons began work on a new building, they employed the same principle as that which is the secret of the assembly line in a factory using the method of mass production. They laid out their work in a series of steps, stages, or degrees so that they would do one thing first and then, because they had done it, could do a second thing and then a third. The separate tasks fell into a series, like the letters in the alphabet. To see beforehand how many steps would be needed and in what order they would come was one of the most difficult and important arts in building. To do that, the Craftsmen had to understand the whole idea and general plan of the building. The building work, therefore, had a serial order.

A building occupied space — if it was to be a cathedral, it might occupy an acre or more. For that reason, it had to be laid out, or planned, spatially—the *where* was as important as the *when*. A stake was set where the cornerstone would be laid; the whole structure was oriented from it. A given wall of a given length was to stand at a certain spot. Each pillar or column was to come at a given point. A door was to be placed here, a window there, an entablature from this point to that point. The base of the tower was to stand so many feet from this and so many feet from that, and this arrangement in space was carried down to a point so fine that any given small piece of mosaic was to have a place of its own. Once these points, positions, and places were fixed in the plans, they came to have a magisterial function because they always dictated where a given workman was to work and what he was to do there. There was a general orientation, and this was so organic that, in most instances, the shifting of one element of the building to another place necessitated a revision of the whole plan. Therefore, the spatial ordering of the structure was a law that the craftsman had to obey. It ordered, or gave orders, to him, and it mattered not if he might prefer to work in one place rather than another because his preferences did not count. As a craftsman, he belonged to an Order because his work was ordered and was so by necessity.

In our modern customs of work, nothing differs more from the customs of work in the Middle Ages than the role of management or superintendence. In modern customs, the superintendent "keeps his distance" in the physical sense and in the sense of his picturing himself as a sort of monarch who issues fiats from a distance. Among Operative Freemasons, both the Master and his Wardens were themselves workmen, reported in at the same time as others, and came through the same apprenticeship; it could never have crossed their minds that they were to stand back giving commands while other men did the work because an idea so puerile had not yet been conceived. They were workmen like other workmen. They worked for wages, worked the same hours, and a craftsman who was superintendent, or Master of Masons, at one place might not be such a one at another, and if so, it was never taken that he had been "demoted."

Where a Master of Masons (or other Officers) differed from other craftsmen was not in the difference between one man who works and another man who "bosses" (Operative Masons would have tolerated no "bosses") but in the difference between a craftsman who did one kind of work and a craftsman who did another kind. It was necessary to send orders to the quarries for stones, their number, kind, and date of delivery; to order them cut and finished by a certain time and in given dimensions; to have some of them carved; to furnish the models or patterns; to see that a carved stone was put in a certain place at a certain time; to coordinate the work being done at one place by one man with work being done (perhaps hundreds of feet away) by another man; to keep records; to pay wages; to employ men as needed and to dismiss them when not needed; to call assemblies and to preside over them; to smooth differences among craftsmen and to resolve their quarrels; and to act as spokesman for the Craft to check on civil authorities or to the administration which employed the men. These functions were themselves forms of work, as toilsome as any other and even more exacting. The officers were craftsmen selected to do those kinds of work, and if Officers had a rank, honors, prerogatives, and powers, it was because the nature of architectural work required that they should have.

In the meantime, a certain number of apprentices were always busy about the place. The fundamental difference between these apprentices and full craftsmen (or "fellows") was that where an adult craftsman was answerable for doing his own work, each apprentice was answerable personally to his own particular Master, and answerable to him only. He was never anything more than a helper. He could decide nothing, undertake nothing on his own initiative, was not responsible for any form of work, and had no voice or vote. His station was, therefore, wholly unlike the status of a Master Craftsman or an Officer.

The whole organization of the Craft thus was made necessary by the work itself. We discuss theories or principles of an organization in the abstract. We prefer someone among the many possible theories such as collective, cooperative, dictatorial, communistic, democratic, etc., and we argue about these as theologians once argued about doctrines. But no Medieval Freemason could even have guessed what these arguments were about because he did not have "theories" or "doctrines," but ordered and arranged, and organized his craft in the form made necessary by the nature of the art of building. If any man had said to him, "But your Craft is not democratic," or "is not monarchic," he would have answered, "What of it?" It was not because he had a "belief" in such a system or had been talked into it by organizers but because the nature of the work (or art) of architecture made such a form of organization necessary. He could not see that he had a choice of having it any other way. There are some of us, even in our talk worn United States, certainly among us Freemasons there are those of us who believe that the Medieval Freemason was far nearer the truth of things than our own schools of economists, our after-dinner speakers, and our newspapers with their catchwords and their propaganda. If there is a certain kind of work that needs to be done if we are to continue to exist, then let us go to work and do it, and if doing it makes it necessary for us to do it in a certain way, then let us do it in that way and not waste our efforts in arguing about the method of doing it.

For such reasons, and in such a sense, Operative Freemasonry was an Order. It was not as if there had been such a thing as Freemasonry beforehand. Freemasonry was itself an Order and was one to begin with. To destroy Freemasonry as an Order would have destroyed Freemasonry. And the Order in which it was during the centuries of its Operative period still exists; there was no change made in respect of that fact in its transition from Operative to Speculative. Every regular lodge in the world is an Order, and no man could make it otherwise without destroying the lodges.

During the twenty years between World Wars I and II, the Fascists (using that word in its most inclusive sense) undertook to set up a single Fascist System in the countries of Europe. Freemasonry was an obstacle, at least, they believed it to be one. They set up an Anti-Masonic organization, with its principal bureau in Paris to remove it. This organization had hundreds of books published to persuade the rank and file of ordinary men that they ought not to be Masons. They accused Freemasonry of many things, but one of the more common of their accusations was to say that Freemasonry is a revolutionary society. They tried to make this plausible by asserting that Freemasonry had plotted the French Revolution and that the Revolutionary motto of "Liberty, Equality, and Fraternity" was the motto of Freemasonry.

This was one of the falsest, or at least one of the most mistaken accusations ever made against Freemasonry, not only because it was mistaken at one point or another but because it was false as a whole. Let's look at this accusation and show why it is not true.

When a Candidate enters the door, he is hoodwinked, cabletowed, and conducted, and from then on, continues to move through the Three Degrees under the narrowest of restraints. Even after he has become a lodge member, and though he may be a lodge member for sixty years, he is always under those same restraints. By "liberty," the French revolutionists meant "without restraint." By "equality," the revolutionists meant the obliteration of status, grades, and ranks. The Fraternity has never believed in doctrinaire libertarianism and never will because it cannot, for libertarianism would abolish half the Landmarks since those Landmarks are in themselves ranks, grades, and differences in status. The Fraternity believes in the free man, an idea far away from libertarianism in its many forms. By "fraternity," the revolutionists meant, "wherever you and I are, we can be brothers together." Such a notion is not at all true of Freemasonry. An Apprentice cannot sit in lodge as the brother of a Fellowcraft, and a Fellowcraft cannot sit in lodge with Master Masons. Only one out of the whole number of members in a lodge can sit in the East, and no Mason can visit or demit to another lodge at his pleasure.

Under the American Constitution, which grants and protects the many rights of free association to its citizens, any number of men can form themselves into a group. They can choose their name, select their officers, and write their own rules. They can be free, each of them, to have a voice about anything, to discuss anything, and to vote about anything. They can, at any time, whenever their whim or circumstances suggest, reorganize, and remodel their organization from top to bottom. They can alter its rules and even wholly change its purposes, which is done in the United States almost every day of the year. But this is never done in a Masonic lodge. Its members cannot say what it is or is not. They cannot make Freemasonry over to suit themselves. If one of them attempts an innovation of the Landmarks, he is reprimanded, suspended, or expelled. What the lodge was before any one of them came into it, it continues to be. It will continue to be that same thing after every one of them has gone. A Candidate cannot take one degree, or seven, or seventy, but must take three, and three only, and he has no voice in what these degrees are, nor has the lodge itself. Once the Candidate has become a member, he has a place or station. He must sit on the sidelines and cannot move at will. Each Officer has a place or station, and only he can occupy it, and he cannot even do that until after he is installed. The Communication of a lodge is at a fixed date and place. It uses fixed rites and ceremonies and conducts its affairs in compliance with its By-Laws and the Order of Business.

The ritual is an orderly arrangement of degrees, rites, ceremonies, steps, and parts, and each symbol comes at a specific place or time. Nothing is fluid or footloose, and nothing is unrestrained. Each member has a voice or a vote about certain things but no voice or vote about other things. The Master is supreme within the jurisdiction of his office and has no authority beyond it. There is no equalitarianism, and neither is there any factionalism or egotism. Within the whole of it, like the skeletal framework in the body of a man, stand the Landmarks, and not even a Grand Lodge can alter them, nor could the whole number of Grand Lodges working together, because, Masonically speaking, they are of the nature of things. It is only another way of saying that Freemasonry is an Order, and anything that contradicts that fact cannot possibly be true.

PART TWO

CHAPTER VII
THE PETITION

Almost every term in the nomenclature of Freemasonry is both ancient and beautiful when defined with knowledge and understanding and correctly used in the times and places to which they belong. They are sound and true; no scientist uses words more accurately. *Petition* is such a word, and since it is more than 3000 years old, the patina of antiquity is upon it. It began as the Latin *peto,* which meant to seek, and became changed into its present form by long usage and by passing from one language to another. It was a sister word of *praetor,* which by usage became transformed into our word prayer. A man prays for something when he desires it greatly. Because he desires it greatly, he seeks it. His petition is his attempt to answer his own prayer.

The 18th Century ritualists who wrote into the ceremonies and rites such changes as were made necessary when Freemasonry was transformed from an Operative (or partly Operative) Fraternity into a Speculative one, and who, about 1750, wrote that portion of the degrees which is called *The Monitor,* left behind a number of phrases, sentences, and paragraphs which are, most of them, easily distinguishable from the older language of the degrees. A microscopic analysis of these phrases and sentences one after another shows that, at many points, these brethren were troubled by what seemed to them to be paradoxes in Freemasonry. Here and there, they betrayed the fact by resorting to odd shifts of thought or language to avoid or resolve them, and not always successfully. Their attempts invite some young Masonic philosophers to devote a career to completing what they began.

A complete list of these paradoxes would be illuminating, but since space forbids making it here, a few must serve as specimens to show what they would be. Why are the members in the Third Degree called Fellowcraft, although they have passed that degree? How do the Fellowcraft in the Second Degree know some things which have not yet occurred and will not until the next degree? If a Candidate is already a man of sound character when he petitions, why have so many moral lessons during the degrees? How can a Petitioner know that he desires to become a Mason when he cannot know what Masonry is until he has received the Three Degrees? If only Masons can know the secrets of Masonry, and if each Mason is under oath never to communicate these secrets to non-Masons, then how are they to be communicated to the Candidate, who is a non-Mason?

Perhaps the most striking of the many paradoxes is enshrined in the old and often-debated question: if only Masons are permitted to enter a lodge when it is duly tiled, how can the Fraternity ever receive new members since no Candidate is a Mason when he enters? Like a score of others, this paradox sounds as if the Fraternity had doomed itself *not* to exist by its own laws. These paradoxes here given are all resolved by the system, which comprises the Petition, Balloting, Preparation, the Ceremony of Entrance, Obligation, Initiation, Passing, and Raising. That system of rules and rites is known collectively as "the making of a Mason." The making of a Mason is the answer to the question: how can the Fraternity accept into membership Masons only when a man cannot be made a Mason outside the Fraternity? It doubles the fascination of the subject of the Petition and the Petitioner when it is studied in its place in this circle of paradoxes. That which generates these paradoxes, or what appear to be paradoxes (the word means "incredibilities"), is the idea, or assumption, that in the eyes of our Fraternity, there are only two categories of men: Masons and non-Masons, whereas in reality there are three. Our brethren in the Middle Ages would have described this third category as a *tertium quid*. Dante described it in his poem as a region that he named *Limbo*. We may describe it in our American language as the class of men who are neither Masons nor non-Masons but are in the process of being made Masons. A Petitioner has taken the first step in that process. He has entered the *Limbo of Masonry*.

We have long been accustomed to thinking that if a thinker solves a great problem, a scientist makes a discovery, or a man accomplishes something great in the arts, their first step will be to give it to the world and give it for nothing. We have even accustomed ourselves to seeing men form large associations and spend great sums of money and time to give something away and to persuade men to accept it. If we who have been thus accustomed to seeing truths given away and to seeing all manner of missionary enterprises financed in the 14th Century, we should naturally expect them not only to open wide the gates of the lodge but also to send out propagandists or missioners. But (and it is another paradox) theirs was the opposite course. They guarded their doors more rigorously than ever. They raised their threshold. They made it more difficult, not less, for new men to enter. They strengthened, not loosened, the obligations and oaths. They sent out no lecturers or missionaries; conducted no campaigns; engineered no propaganda, published no books, asked no clergymen to preach for them, and requested no schools to put Freemasonry into the curriculum. Never in history has any organization with something new and great for the world done less to have it accepted or shown more indifference to what the world thought or said about it. The fact is more than wonderful; it is amazing, and no other fact about Freemasonry is more striking or revealing.

A man petitions to receive the Three Degrees. It will not be until after he has successfully surmounted those three barriers that he can take the last step of petitioning for membership in a lodge. No man can decide to become a Mason; he can only petition because membership is no man's right. It is conferred, but it is not offered. He must fill in a printed official form and sign it with his legal name and by his own hand – an "X" will not be accepted. He must be of lawful age. He must be a man, must be well recommended, and he must have his petition signed by men who are Masons. The qualifications required of him are not qualifications in general. Many men are highly qualified for many vocations – but he must have just those qualifications which are called for in Masonic work. He must put a certain sum ("initiation fee") in escrow with the lodge. He must come of his own free will. The "free" means that he is free to act without consulting others and is committed to no obligations that will conflict with his Masonic obligations. The "will" does not mean he wills something in general but wills to be a Mason. He is not to be solicited; he is to solicit no Mason to vote for him when he passes the ordeal of the ballot. Once he has signed his petition and mailed it to the Secretary, he is to wait patiently and remain circumspection until he hears from the lodge.

Such a Petitioner is not a member, a half-member, or a prospective member. He is not even a Candidate until he has passed a favorable ballot. Nevertheless, he has a status, and though it is not inside Freemasonry, it is *officially recognized* by Freemasonry and comes under its rules and regulations. He cannot attend a lodge, appeal to a lodge, or have any voice there. A lodge is never under any obligation even to accept his petition for consideration, investigate it, or bring it to the ballot. A lodge can return it to him without warning, excuse, or argument. He is wholly and solely in the position of one who prays, seeks, or asks. And he is doing so with no encouragement except from his internal desires. Therefore, he must not take it amiss if the door is not opened when he knocks. If his petition is returned to him without ballot or is rejected by an unfavorable ballot, he stands where he stood before. He has done no harm to himself.

Somewhere in or about London, or possibly at York, and near the year 1350, the Freemasons in a lodge decided not to dissolve their lodge when their work was completed but to keep it as a permanent center of Freemasonry. They rested their authority for doing so upon the first written copy of the Old Charges. Men who sought membership in it, as Operatives or Speculatives (Accepted), had to petition as a man does now; and it was no easier then than it is now for them to pass the ordeal of the ballot and afterward to be made a Mason — if anything it was even more difficult. The lodge — and we do not know its name or town — was doubtless a small one of fifteen to thirty members. After a time, a second lodge was constituted on the same authority, and as time passed, one after another was set up here and there in England, Scotland, and Ireland. Not one of those lodges solicited members, sent out agents, salesmen, or missionaries, or advertised itself, but gave everywhere the impression that accepting a new member was almost the last thing it wished to do. Wherefrom two questions arise: how did the Fraternity survive, through thick and thin, and across six centuries? And how can we explain its immense vitality, its irrepressible growth into a Fraternity of millions of men established in fifty or sixty countries and speaking forty or fifty languages? It put forth no effort either to survive or to grow. Why did it?

Each and every petitioner has the answer in his own hand, not only in the printed form but also as the petition is recalled to him during the degrees. It is in that statement which Grand Jurisdictions word differently but which in meaning is everywhere the same. And which is to the effect that the petitioner was moved to pray for the honor of receiving the degrees by Freemasonry's good name, its repute, and its reputation for both antiquity and honor. An old and wise interpreter of the ritual once declared this "to be the most beautiful fact in Masonry" and explained that it was beautiful because Freemasonry had never said it about itself. If it has never said it about itself, then others have said it for Freemasonry. The petitioner must come of his own free will; this reputation also arose of its own free will. It came of itself. It arose around the Fraternity without prompting and, as it were, as grass and shrubs do, grew up out of the ground without any man's planting. This free, universal, and unbought testimony is responsible for that longevity and growth. Has any society, fraternity, or association ever received a larger testimony?

CHAPTER VIII
THE SYMBOLIC DEGREES

A candidate learns what a degree is twice over, once while it is being conferred upon him and again when he learns it by heart. He discovers that nothing is indefinite about any of them because each begins at a fixed moment, at a specified place, with a given action, then proceeds in a fixed order until it comes to a clean-cut end with a given action, at a given place. There is no ambiguity or uncertainty in it, nothing extemporized. It is as definitely cut and patterned as a diamond.

Where did Freemasons find the idea of a degree? How did they come to adopt degrees as the means for making a Mason? Those questions call for long answers, but the first can be compressed into the statement that they found the idea nowhere and did not consciously adopt degrees to make Masons. Degrees seem to have arisen of themselves, one bit at a time and came almost unintentionally and accidentally. The Operative Freemasons, out of whose practices the degrees were made, never heard of a degree, and had none. For this reason, a complete history of the degrees cannot be written except in the form of a complete history of Freemasonry.

A degree is a single organized system of rites and ceremonies. Although not mentioned in our two oldest documents, the *Regius* and the *Cooke MSS.*, they make sharp distinctions among Apprentices, Fellows, and Lodge Officers. In all probability, degrees came into first use in the 17th Century. Although the elements or rites or ceremonies incorporated in them were much older. There is mention of our present penalties as used in our Third Degree in 1700. We also know that the lodges conferred only two degrees when the Mother Grand Lodge was constituted in 1717. It is likely that the formation of degrees had its first germ in the acceptance of non-Operative (Speculative) members by Operative Lodges (probably in the latter half of the 14th Century). Degrees are almost the only possible means by which the old Operative practices, rules, regulations, rites, and ceremonies could have been put to new use by the Speculative Freemasons.

From the discovery of the *Regius MS.* in 1838 until Gould began writing his *History* about 1870, the majority of Masonic scholars, with W. J. Hughan as their leader, believed that before the Grand Lodge of 1717, lodges had conferred only one degree. Gould set up a powerful argument favoring the theory that they had conferred two degrees. At the time of this writing, three-quarters of a century after Gould, a circle of scholars believe that lodges before 1717 conferred three degrees. The debate has been a long one and has been so thoroughly discussed that except for the subject of the Old Charges, more Masonic learning has gone into the discussion than into any other single question in our history.

It is now beginning to appear that the debate will be transformed by bringing to bear upon it a new set of ideas in which the question of one, two, or three degrees will lose meaning. The principal one among these new ideas derives from the fact that before 1717 (and possibly as late as 1740), Freemasons did not think in terms of degrees but in terms of lodges. It was a Lodge of Apprentices into which a Candidate was first initiated, not a degree; and so with Fellows and Masters.

Historical facts support this hypothesis, but even if we had no historical facts, any reasonable analysis of Speculative practices would support it. This would be because, to this day, an Apprentice does not become a member of an Apprentice Degree but of an Apprentice Lodge, and so with Fellows and Masters. A lodge uses degrees but consists of many things besides its degrees. There could therefore have been Lodges of Apprentices and Lodges of Fellows long before any degrees of Apprentices or Fellows existed. Either of those lodges could have used a greater or a lesser amount of obligations, charges, lectures, modes of identification, rites, or ceremonies but could have used them unorganized. No two lodges needed to use them in the same order or the same amount. To sum up, there were probably Lodges of Apprentices and Lodges of Fellows long before there were degrees by those names, using "degree" in the sense of an organized system of rites.

If this is an accurate account of the history of the degrees, did Masons have two lodges or one lodge before 1717? Before this question can be answered, we must consider the often-overlooked fact that we currently have not three lodges (one for each degree) in Ancient Craft Masonry but *four*. Although to make this accurate, the word "lodge" is used in the fourth instance with a meaning not quite the same as in the other instances. We have the regular, chartered lodge which can meet monthly or semi-monthly without conferring any degrees — it is what almost every Mason means by "the lodge." It should be noted that this chartered lodge consists of its members only. Master Masons (Raised to the Third Degree) belonging to other lodges are not members of this lodge until they join it. If this chartered lodge is called "a lodge" (as it should be), then when it is added to the Lodge of Apprentices and the Lodge of Fellows, and the Lodge of Masters, it makes a total of four lodges. If we count the chartered lodge as a fourth lodge and continue to think of it in that same sense, there must have been three lodges before 1717 – the Lodge of Apprentices, the Lodge of Fellows (also called Master Mason), and the regular permanent lodge which could meet and transact business without conferring degrees. W. J. Hughan's theory of only one degree before 1717 meant that (according to him) a regular local lodge met to make a Mason and did so in a single sitting. Why could Hughan's colleagues not accept this theory? Because it was unthinkable that three or four, or five Apprentices could have been permitted to remain in lodge while Candidates were receiving the Obligations, Modes of Identification, and other secrets belonging to Fellows of the Craft (or Master Masons; the two names meant the same thing then). Even when Candidates were Entered as Apprentices and made Fellows ("Raised") in one evening, the brethren had to open a Lodge of Apprentices, Enter the Apprentices, close it, open a Lodge of Fellows, etc. (Even if the rites and ceremonies used then were not organized and crystallized into single units, or degrees, as now).

As the earth's geological history is discoverable from the elements now making up its surface, so is the history of the degrees written in their composed material. Somewhat cryptically, the jig-saw pieces needing to be fitted together become clear upon analysis. No degree is composed of forms or formality; it is not even composed, except in parts, of symbols and ceremonies. It also has in it much law, several possible things (such as the Modes of Recognition), teachings, charges, lectures, instructions, clothing, money, etc. At some points, it is completely symbolic. At other points, it is wholly literal. The Secretary and the Treasurer have a place in it as well as the Master and his Wardens. It is more like a world than it is like an essay, a play, or a lecture. We say that a degree is conferred on a Candidate or that he "takes it." In reality, he enters a lodge (of Apprentices, Fellows, or Masters), and the degree is only a part of that lodge.

We Americans are so tangled up in our complexities and the size of the population, and the size and variety of our country that we find ourselves always talking wholesale with words such as labor, capital, politics, isolationism, internationalism, prosperity, etc. We offer large words, empty as the sky, dry, abstract, and difficult to absorb ceremonies to bear on any "John Jones." Like other men in the Middle Ages, the Operative Freemasons had none of these sweeping and universal abstractions. If we were to attempt to recover the use of apprenticeship in our country (as we ought to do), we should immediately begin to call it the apprenticeship system. The Medieval Masons did not think of it as a system, nor did they discuss its general and abstract merits. When a youth of twelve or so, with his father's consent, asked to be taught the art of architecture, the Freemasons did not say, "Here is another specimen; give him number 128, 932, 465." Nor did they drop him into an impersonal mill where he vanished from view except in the disguise of some indistinguishable unit among the ten thousand other indistinguishable units. To them, he was Robin. He came from near Essex. His father was a yeoman farmer on the estate of Sir Montmorency Clittenhouse. They looked him over. They looked him in the eyes. Their question was how to make a Freemason out of this boy. They refused to bind him as an apprentice to some Master until they were sure he would be happy with that particular boy.

Such a boy was investigated and examined and stood up before the lodge. He was charged. The King's government had found, declared, and promulgated laws to protect and regulate just such boys, and the lodge had to be mindful of those laws. The boy was given an oath or obligation. He was given such secrets as belonged to his status. He was indentured to one of the Master Masons in the lodge, and that Master took the boy home with him, gave him clothes, supplied him with a few tools, took him into the family, and introduced him to the neighbors. He had to teach him everything there was to be learned about the art of architecture. And from then on, the boy was a member of the Masonic Community. According to the *Regius MS.*, such a boy remained in apprenticeship for seven years. If he entered an apprenticeship in a lodge with a membership of fifty or sixty, employed on a large building which would take ten to twenty years to complete, he would find eight or ten other boys in the lodge at various stages of their terms of apprenticeship.

The life and career of an Operative Apprentice were not shortened to one night, nor could the many actions of the lodge concerned with him have been reduced to one organized degree; what he had was not a degree but a status. Since such a youth was the lodge's ward and was present for work during the same hours as the Master Masons, it is inconceivable that the lodge officially was finished with him after he had taken his obligation and his name had been entered on the books. There must have been many occasions for him to be in lodge alone or with his fellow apprentices. He would be called before his elders if any questions arose regarding his well-being, skill, or conduct. And in the many ceremonies, processions, feast days, etc., he and his fellow apprentices had parts, places, and their own costumes. The lodge also had a body of rules for their regulation and guidance.

It was this status, and everything connected with it, which was permanent and unchangeable in the Fraternity. Around this status, there began, probably in the 14th Century, to gather an organized body of rites, ceremonies, rules, and symbols. Once the lodges had become wholly Speculative, these ceremonies rapidly crystallized into the present Entered Apprentice Degree. With its words, phrases, and actions, that degree as we now have it would possibly be unrecognizable to a Master Mason brought back from a 12th Century grave. And yet, at the same time, he would instantly recognize certain things in it because its theme is apprenticeship, and he had seven years to learn that theme.

In one of our lodges, a Candidate usually is a stranger to most when he arrives for his initiation. When he takes his Second Degree two or four weeks later, he continues to be almost a stranger. In Operative Freemasonry, it was far otherwise. After seven years, every fellow craftsman knew him as well as he knew himself. In the home of his own Master, he had by now become almost a foster son.

Meanwhile, he had enjoyed fellowship with many Freemasons traveling through or stopping off for temporary work (there were many specialists in the Craft). From there, he had his first-hand report about cities he had never seen and countries of which he had never heard. It was no stranger who entered the lodge at the end of his apprenticeship to be given his test of skill in the form of a Master's piece. The reports made about him were reports about someone well known. And then, if all were favorable, he was to be given the oath of a Fellow, which made him a member of the lodge. Insofar as he had learned everything about the work during his tutelage and had mastered his skill, he was called a Master Mason. He was now a full-fledged member, was given a new status, could work for wages, and have his own apprentices. He could have a vote, a voice, and could hold office. He was called a *Fellow of the Craft*.

In his case, as in the Apprentice, his relation to the Craft and the lodge could not be summed up in a single degree or completed in one evening. His relationship with the lodge and its members was spread over many years. It took the form of the many duties, rights, privileges, prerogatives, rules, regulations, and obligations which went along with his status. And, once again, this status remained unchanged until the 18th Century, and the many elements belonging to it were the materials out of which the Second Degree became crystallized.

This culmination of his full membership in the Second Degree in lodges until well toward the middle of the 18th Century is puzzling. It may even perplex Freemasons who, from their first day and ever since, have not known nor heard of any Ancient Craft Masonry except in three degrees. It also was a puzzle to our Speculative forbears who, about 1740, added on a new, or Third degree because they had to disturb much in the old Second Degree to add it, and the raw sutures have never healed. Such solecisms as the symbolism inside the Middle Chamber in the Second Degree and the appearance of Fellowcraft in the Third Degree are instances of the impossibility of reorganizing the System without falling into inconsistency in detail. The brethren at the time could not reorganize everything. They did the best they could.

On the engraved List of Lodges issued by the Mother Grand Lodge in 1725, a "Masters' Lodge" appears for the first time. Others were to follow during the next decade, and many others were constituted (as we can discover from lodge Minutes) which did not appear on the Lists. Although this new type of lodge apparently had no predecessors, it appeared late in Masonic history and at the capital of the then Masonic world. Although it was to have a revolutionizing effect upon Speculative Freemasonry, surprisingly little is known about them. This is partly because nothing of any ritual was written or printed even by lodge Secretaries and partly because Masters' Lodges appear to have kept themselves almost hidden from sight. By adding together such data as we have, correlating them with others known by facts about the Fraternity at the time, and using reasoning, there is good ground for believing that the following statements of facts are dependable.

1. In the beginning, Masters' Lodges consisted of Masters or Past Masters, which were variously styled Past, Passed, or Pass Masters. Later it appears that any experienced Craftsman, acceptable to a Masters' Lodge, could petition for membership provided he took some oath, pledge, or ceremony – perhaps this was the origin of the phrase "Virtual Past Masters."

2. A Masters' Lodge met separately from regularly chartered lodges and often held communications on Sunday afternoons. They might meet in a room of their own, or a room adjacent to a Lodge Room, or might use a regular Lodge Room when the lodge owning it was not in Communication. How many existed is not known. It is impossible to guess, but as the middle of the century approached (1740-1750), their number must have greatly increased.

3. One lodge after another began to incorporate a Master's Lodge into itself (the lodges of the Ancient Grand Lodge appear to have done so from the beginning) until finally, it had become the standard in practice. When this was done, the Masters' Lodge became the Third Degree.

4. The indications are that the Ritual of a Masters' Lodge included, at least in part, what later became organized as the Royal Arch Degree. This degree was a Side Degree connected with lodges until separate Chapters and Grand Chapters were organized. This doubtless explains why the Ancient Grand Lodge continued to insist that the Royal Arch was an integral part of Ancient Craft

Masonry, and with such tenacity that as late as the Union in 1813, it forced through a resolution to the effect that Ancient Craft Masonry consists of the Three Degrees and the Holy Royal Arch. It is possible that the portion of the Third Degree called, *The Raising*, and of which HA.·. is the center, may originally have belonged to a single degree of which the Royal Arch Degree was also a part. If that were true, the long search for the origin of the *Rite of the Raising* (HA.·.), which has always failed, may have failed because the searchers should have been seeking the origin of a Rite of a different kind. Also, the fact that a Masters' Lodge was first mentioned in 1725 does not fix the earliest possible date. Years before that date, in England and Ireland, there were a number of Masonic Side Orders, and it may be that the first Masters' Lodge was one of those Side Orders turning itself into a lodge. It may have been used a century before 1725 as a Side Order. A reference to Penalties in 1700 suggests that the central ceremony may have been older than that date.

5. The work, duties, powers, prerogatives, and privileges of officers in Operative Lodges, even at the earliest date and in lodges the most temporary, gave officers a status, unlike the status of either Fellows or Apprentices. The Master ruled and governed in literal fact; under some circumstances, he wielded authority now exclusively reserved for a civil government. His Wardens belonged to the same category as himself because it was their function to assist him in ruling and governing (this ignores differences in the names of offices then and now). The Secretary was responsible for keeping the books and the Treasurer for keeping the funds. Their duties were not confined to the work or the lodge but extended to the whole Community. Around the status of Officers, there grew up as many ceremonies, rites, symbols, rules, regulations, etc., as around the status of Fellows or Apprentices. With all its ramifications, this status of

Officers was a Landmark and has been preserved or has persisted ever since. The Third Degree, as a degree, is an organized system of rites and ceremonies that crystallize the status of Officers, and that status is the theme of the degree. Instead of being called Master Mason Degree, it ought to be called Master of Masons Degree because it is a drama of government. It is not the Craft or the Building around which the degree revolves but about the Master of Masons.

CHAPTER IX
SYMBOLS AND SYMBOLISM

The sun, as it shines full, and at the top of the day, is as real, actual, and material as anything can be. An artist drawing a decoration for the wall of a room could represent the sun with a golden circle. Such a circle would be a symbol. But a writer could eliminate even the diagrammatic circle and use the sun as a symbol by letting it stand for anything that gives light. In neither event would the symbolist turn the sun into anything other than itself. The sun would be the same actual and material sun after this symbolic use of it that it had been before; if it did not, the symbols would lose their meaning.

Rifles in the hands of a squad of soldiers are used as practical, literal weapons in warfare. If the same rifles are fired by the same squad of soldiers at a soldier's burial, they are used symbolically. The act of firing has become a symbolic act. We know from literature, music, painting, sculpture, and ritual that almost anything can be put to symbolic uses, and almost everything has been. There is scarcely an object, event, tool, or experience which has not been used for symbolic purposes. A gnarled old man hoeing his turnips is nothing but a man hoeing his turnips, but he is also the painting "Man with a Hoe," a symbol of labor. A symbol, therefore, is like the earth's path around the sun, an ellipse about the poles, one of them being the actual, literal, real thing itself, the other the meanings it has that go beyond itself and may be carried elsewhere. It is always false symbology to suppose that when a thing is used symbolically, it has been made unreal and turned into a species of make-believe.

A symbol may be any of a large number of objects, pictures, diagrams, etc. As such, it may have a form wholly unlike the thing it represents. When a sword is used as a symbol of war, it does not look like a war scene. A sign in a Medieval town with a bed on it would likely mean that a traveler has found an inn. A sign with a frothy mug of ale would mean a tavern. The symbol's meaning must be true of the thing used, or the symbol is false. But even so, why use symbols? Well, because they are so convenient. There also was a time when the ability to read was rare. A sign with a mug of ale might be understood where the word "tavern" would mean nothing. A given thing must have an easy to understand and remember meaning. One goes to an inn to sleep, and you sleep in a bed, so a sign with a bed on it is easy and clear. Also, the meaning of one thing may be found again in many other things. Thus, using a pair of scales to symbolize weight might also symbolize justice – as in weighing the truth or falseness of something. There is nothing strained, odd, or exceptional in using symbols. Symbols are as familiar as gestures and as universal as languages. Alfred N. Whitehead, who had one of the best intellects of the 20th Century, and was co-author with Bertrand Russell of *Principia Mathematica,* was so impressed by the universality of the use of symbolism that he built a whole system of philosophy around it.

Nothing is more difficult for a symbologist to understand than the notion that it is the function of a symbol to make its meaning secret. It is the function of a symbol to express a truth, not to be mute about it. The point of a symbol is to reveal meaning easily and simply, not to conceal it. It is to say something, not to keep silent about it. Unless a symbol can make some fact or idea more evident and easier to comprehend, it has failed in its purpose and is a false one. Yes, one might expect that a tavern might have tables and chairs for customers to sit. But a sign with a chair on it would not be a good symbol for a tavern. It is neither clear nor easy to understand.

What is the meaning of a symbol? A symbol is normally understood as an object, picture, device, etc., which is used to represent something else. The meaning is never found in the symbol but in what it represents. Freemasons understand the Letter G as a symbol of Geometry. An ingenious theorist could write a book about the letter G, its history, shape, etc., and collect hundreds of myths, legends, and tales about it. But the meaning of G as the seventh letter of the alphabet is not that of the Masonic understanding of *The Letter G* as a symbol.

Many things used in symbology are so rich that many meanings may represent them, or one symbol may be used for many purposes. An instance is the moon. A long and varied list of figures and pictures, such as Moses, a goddess, a hunchback, a prophet, a Queen of Night, a scimitar, the night-time, etc., has symbolized the moon. The North (or Polar) Star is an instance of the second case. The swastika has been used as a symbol for at least 4,000 years, and Count Goblet d' Alviela believed it to be the oldest symbol still in use—long before the Nazis perverted it. Many people and religions have employed the swastika for at least a hundred purposes. For this reason, one of the first rules of symbology is that any given symbol must be interpreted in its context and in the light of the purpose for which it is used.

Whether a symbol represents one meaning or many, the meanings belong to it. The interpreter's function is not to give meanings to the symbol but to find the meanings already there. They are not *his* meanings, but the symbol's meanings. No mathematician would dream of giving the number 9 any value he may fancy. Outside of mathematics, someone may use the number 9 as a symbol for anything that they chose, but within mathematics we are bound to its one, original meaning. An interpreter of a symbol is equally bound. He cannot read into the symbol, fashion for it, or attribute any meaning not already its own. The compasses are a symbol. They represent a circle. It may be any circle, a geometrician's, an artist's, a hostess's circle of guests, the sky, or the horizon (a circle of which a man can see only an arc). There are many uses of the circle, and each use means something. But any symbolic interpretation of the circle that is misleading to the facts and properties of a circle is false. The doctrine sometimes heard, even in Lodge Rooms, which says, "You can give a symbol any meaning you choose," is false.

Freemasonry is probably the world's most magnificent masterpiece of symbolism. I believe that it is more symbolic from top to bottom, is richer in symbols of every type, has a larger number of them, and has carried symbology nearer to perfection than any other association. For a man who responds to symbols as a musician responds to music, it has an infinite, never-wearying fascination. And if he gives his career to it, he is not throwing his life away. He will find in its many symbolisms a work by masters in this art. They are sublime, of profound meaning, inexhaustibly rich, and of that great beauty that is never found except in the supreme masterpieces. And if he does pursue it, he will find in it, and at work, the whole complement of principles and rules which comprise his art. Freemasonry could not be a great system of symbolism if he didn't. Symbolism is, in this respect, like a circle. Either it is perfect, or it does not exist. This chapter's explanation and rules of symbology can be superimposed upon Freemasonry and will furnish a Newly-Made Mason with a guide to the ritual.

It was widely believed, a century ago, that Operative Freemasonry came to a virtual end in about the 16th Century. It was believed that in the Transition Period, new growths began to spring up among the Operative ruins; and that in 1717 these suddenly flowered into a new kind of Freemasonry. What occurred during that long history of the Fraternity occurred in another region and was wholly different from that. The ancient, time-immemorial Operative Fraternity was preserved intact. During the Transition Period, each new member, Operative or Accepted, pledged never to be guilty of introducing innovations into the Fraternity. Today we continue to give that same pledge. The only significant and fundamental change was to put the ancient Operative Fraternity to new use. That new use would have been pointless had the old Fraternity not remained there to be used. This putting the old Freemasonry to a new use was the only transition from Operative Freemasonry to our Speculative Freemasonry. When we say that Speculative Freemasonry is Symbolic Freemasonry, it is that new use which is meant. But Symbolic Freemasonry is not the whole of Speculative Freemasonry. Many customs, usages, Landmarks, and laws are not symbolic but are still as literal and "operative" as they were eight centuries ago. Only that which is presented, shown, or taught in the Fraternity utilizing symbols belongs to Symbolic Masonry.

In each instance, the many symbols in our Ancient Craft Masonry are wholly Masonic. They are part of the teachings, the education, of Freemasons. There is no guarantee that any symbol used outside of Freemasonry has the same, or any, meaning inside of Freemasonry. Masons cannot bring the meanings of symbols found elsewhere back into Freemasonry because every Masonic symbol has a use and a meaning exclusively its own. Nor can Masons take our meanings of symbols and insist that it is the meaning for others. Yes, in Medieval times it is very possible that taverns in distant towns, and ones who never encountered each other, used signs with mugs of ale to inform travelers that this was a tavern. Each was free to use whatever symbol they chose and they, by chance, used the same symbol. This does not mean that a mug of ale is the only symbol that could be used for a tavern, nor that a mug of ale can *only* be understood to mean a tavern. Symbols must be valid and true for the ones using them.

It is Freemasonry itself that uses its own symbols and decides what symbols it is to use. What ideas, facts, or teachings it may express by means of them is not for any outside fraternity, organization, or religion to decide. Let other associations have their own symbols and use them for their own purposes. We contend they should always be free to do so because it is what we do ourselves. Their symbols, and the meanings of their symbols, are useful and valid for them. Thousands of symbols are sown throughout the Old and New Testaments, in the Koran, the Zend Avesta, the Vedas, and Kabbalism. Alchemy, Rosicrucianism, and other forms of Medieval hermeticism are not our symbols, and their meanings have nothing to do with the meaning of our ritual. Any symbol in the Three Degrees is a Masonic Symbol, and it can be interpreted only in terms of its Masonic use — that is, the first law, the great Landmark of Masonic symbology. If some symbol we use has a meaning that is shared by any other, then this does not mean that *all* ours and theirs are the same.

Each of our many symbols can be traced back to some period in our history when a practice or custom in the Craft work came to be used to present something or say something of educational value to Masons. They became symbols of themselves, therefore, and without exception, originated historically. That fact includes that each symbol has a history of its own, and it is often by means of its history and long-continued use that it can be best explained.

PART THREE

CHAPTER X
GREAT SYMBOLS

1st Group
The Lodge – Working Tools – The Altar – Square and Compasses

There is no support in the history, Landmarks, regulations, rules, or teachings for the theory that Freemasonry uses symbols to hide or disguise its lessons. They are used to *say* something. They are never used for *not* saying it. If a stranger stops to ask directions, the man he asks may put his reply in words or point with his finger. If he uses the sign instead of the words, it is not because he has taken a sudden whim to refuse the request or to make it a mystery. There are circumstances under which a sign or a symbol can speak even more clearly than words. If an American in a French village inquires his way, the villager will point rather than speak because the American may not know the French language. There are some 200 symbols, emblems, allegories, signs, and ceremonies in the Three Degrees. Not one of them is to conceal anything or mystify anyone, but they are there for the opposite purpose of making clear, of making plain, of showing, of stating, of saying.

1. ***The Lodge***. A lodge is a body of Masons so organized that they move and work together as if many had but one body. The Operative Freemasons needed to work together as a body because they were engaged in the same task, at the same time, and under one supervision. They knew that nowhere, nor under any circumstances, could the type of buildings they constructed be erected if each man worked independently. Nor was it a mystery that they had a private room set aside for themselves because they had to

plan together, decide together, learn their designs together, and receive instructions for their labor at one time and all together. Insofar as they labored in such a manner, we do so also in Speculative Freemasonry because ours is the same lodge model as theirs. If we say that it is a symbolic lodge, it is not because we have turned the lodge into a symbol but because we, as Speculative Masons, do not use the tools of the Operatives in the same manner as they Masons did. We labor in our lodges by symbolic use of the tools of the operatives. The goal of Speculative Lodges is not the construction of physical buildings, but the education and moral/social improvement of the Members.

2. ***Working Tools.*** They are the tools, implements, and instruments by which things are made and measured, and produced. If a man cannot live without houses, food, clothing, schools, governments, medicine, and arts, then he cannot live without tools because nowhere in nature or man do these things come ready-made. In life, there is such a variety of species of plants and animals that a biologist can scarcely catalog them. The mind faints as it envisages how many have lived in the past but live no more and will live in the future but not yet. But nowhere in that fathomless fertility is there a way for a pair of shoes to be grown, or a suit of clothes to be harvested out of the back of a sheep, or for meat to cook itself. "Wherever anything is at all, physical matter is there," it has many ways for species of things to exist as life has ways found a way to live. But in the whole of it, there is no way for buildings, airplanes, or automobiles to come into existence by themselves. Man also has within his potentiality a variety as illimitable as life or as matter. But unlike life, men do not come in species; unlike matter, one man is never replaceable by another. If there are now billions of men and women in the world, no two are alike, not even remotely so, and each one is as absolutely and uniquely himself as if he were the only man alive. For all that, men do not come

into being already able to read, write, speak, or work — no infant has been a farmer, a merchant, a doctor, a teacher, or an architect at birth. As far as he is concerned, man is as helpless to make or produce the things without which he cannot continue to be as is either life or matter. He must have tools to make or produce those things, or he will perish — the statement of that fact could be neither spoken nor even written without using instruments and devices.

Tools belong to what he is, and the tools in his hand belong as much to him as the teeth in his head. Tools are, therefore, not extraneous to man, detachable, accidental, or incidental, as if he could lay them down or take them up when he might fancy. If a man becomes so superior in some dream of himself that he becomes "too good for himself" and is so superior that he despises his own eyes, nose, stomach, or feet, he is insane. He is equally irrational if he becomes childish enough to consider himself superior to the use of tools, or that he is socially above them, or that because of his caste, he must not soil his hands on them, for that is the way where starvation lies.

The Working Tools of the ritual are these same tools of wood and metal, without which no man can long continue to be a man. They are not mystical pictures of ineffable ideas. The Gauge is an ordinary measuring stick, with inches marked upon it, and not a "symbol" of some metaphysical mystery like time. The Gavel is not a "symbol" of "Moses' hammer," nor of any occult or esoteric doctrine, but is a heavy iron tool, with a square head on one side for pounding stone and an edge on the other for cutting it. The Trowel is not "a picture of the Mystic Tie." It has no remote connection with the Mystic Tie. Any Operative Freemason who ever lived would have laughed at such notions. The Trowel is the tool for spreading or pointing mortar, plaster, and cement. These are used symbolically in the Speculative Mason's Ritual, not in the sense that they are explained away or turned into something other than themselves. They are used in the sense that, while in Operative Freemasonry, they were used by builders, in Speculative Freemasonry, they are not only used by builders but also represent all tools everywhere, of every kind. They belong to work and belong to its necessity, and therefore belong to Man in his capacity as a worker, and also, in an equal necessity, they belong to Freemasonry's philosophy of work and moral development. In that philosophy is the doctrine, "If thou wouldst be a man, thou must be a user of tools, therefore learn to use them." And the Ceremony of Presentation of the Tools to an Apprentice is an acted-out statement of that doctrine. "If thou, young man, feel thyself to be superior to the use of tools, if thou art one who refuses to lift the stone because thou shouldest have to stoop in order to lift it, thou art not qualified to be one of us. No youth is worthy to be a Candidate for Manhood unless he is proud to accept his own kit of tools and is willing to toil for his seven years in learning to use them."

3. ***The Altar***. If anything in any Lodge Room appears to be remote from daily work, from the plow in the soil, from the ax in the tree, from the gavel on the stone, it is the Altar. It may be remote in appearance; it is not so in reality. It is not a theological Altar but a craft Altar. On it lies not a book of specific theology but the Book of the Law. Also lying on it, and with equal sanctity, are the Square and Compasses, the emblem of the Craft of Masonry. In the Operative Lodge Room, it was the place where the Apprentice came both to stand and to kneel when he gave his promise to obey the Rules and Regulations and put himself in pledge as a guarantee of his promise. He gave his oath, which was his reputation as a man that he would learn his trade thoroughly. He promised that he could be depended on to be at his place where his work called him, that his fellows could rely on him not to fail them. He

swore he would never leave them in the lurch and would be a good citizen under the Government of his Craft.

In the nature of things, a man who cannot be depended on can have no place in work. It is impossible to police every man. It is impossible to have a Master of Masons to supervise each Mason as it would be to give each workman anywhere else a private foreman or to assign him a private instructor to show him at each turn what to do and how to do it. He must supervise himself, must give himself his orders and instructions. He must inspect himself, judge himself, and govern himself. He must do so, or he cannot work because there are in the nature of things no way possible to do such things for him. He is obliged, and a stern one, whether it is painful to him or not. The Altar means that he is under that obligation if he is a Mason. It also means that he is equal, so if he is a farmer, doctor, miner, clerk, or teacher, it matters not as to his worldly profession. He has his Craft, whatever he is, his own Square and Compasses. His Craft has its own laws, rules, and regulations and *Book of Constitutions*. The *Volume of the Law* and the Square and Compasses are not in the center of the Lodge Room because of any peculiarity of Masonry. They are there because they are also necessarily there because no form of work can go on without them.

4. ***The Square and Compasses***. In the Middle Ages, each Craft and guild used a trademark, hallmark, emblem, or device to identify itself as a flag. Since so few men could read or write, the quarters of a town, a market, a shop, or a hall were always marked by a picture, a statue, or a carving. Even as late as the end of the 18th Century, inns and taverns continued to be called by the pictures on their signs. The Goose and Gridiron Alehouse was so named because its sign was a picture of Apollo's swan and lyre. The Square and Compasses were the device, sign, or emblem that stood everywhere for the Craft of Architecture or Freemasonry—it even appears in churches

and cathedrals in "the Mason's window." As used on the Altar in their capacity of Great Lights, along with the *Volume of the Law,* they are not used as Working Tools (or, rather, working instruments) but as an emblem of the Craft of Freemasonry. The Craft, its work, and its laws are the great light for every Apprentice. It is that which he is to see. It is that by which he is to see, and his schooling and his training will be to throw light on every detail of his work in the Craft. It is in that Craft, and to that Craft, that he stands in obligation and takes his obligations. This means that when the Candidate is admitted to membership, as he is by taking the obligation, it is not into work at large that he is admitted, but into the particular kind of work done by builders. It is not merely into a lodge that he is admitted but into the Craft. Henceforth he will be a craftsman under the aegis of the Square and Compasses.

Does any Candidate for training in work enter a craft? He does. If a man stops to think it through, this fact is one of the most surprising and profound facts, and it is a mystery why it is so seldom seen. There is no such thing as "work at wholesale," "work at large," or "mere work." Any work, any kind or form, is invariably divided into crafts, and an apprentice or beginner is always admitted into "this particular work." It is a very large fact about man and ought to be studied as one of the major subjects in both economics and sociology. It not only means that for every man in the world, of any language or color, work is the only means by which he can sustain himself. It also means that work is everywhere in a number of species or forms — in our Masonic nomenclature, it is divided into crafts. It is divided into trades, callings, arts, and professions and is so necessary and universal, and any youth who enters work must enter it through the doors of one of those crafts. He can never become a worker unless he is willing to learn the duties and techniques of some given craft. The Apprentice knocking at the Inner Door of the Masonic lodge is the complete, perfect picture of the Apprentice anywhere. He must find some particular lodge, knock on some particular door, and enter some particular craft.

We men and women are born into a world which is not a welter, and still less a chaos, but one which has, as it were, an anatomy of its own. If ever the earth itself was void and without form, it must have been an awfully long time ago because no traces remain of that condition of flux. The earth is so accurate in its motions that we set our watches by day and night, and the months and the seasons are equally regular. Even the weather would be predictable down to the last detail if we knew enough about it. Nor are animals and plants less ordered. They are born into kinds, families, species, and varieties. Is man equally predictable? It can be predicted that men will always decide some things for themselves and perhaps decide them wrong. It also can be predicted that men will be active in some things and will always have shelters or houses, food, heat, clothing, medicine, schooling, furniture, belongings, and many other things. To have these things, men will always have to set up a correspondence between the kinds of things they use and the kinds of species of material things, animals, and plants that they will find in the world outside.

It is, therefore, a combination of the nature of man with the nature of the world, which predestines us for all time to divide our work into crafts. A craft is nothing other than a form of work made necessary by a man's needing a certain kind and the world having materials of a certain kind by which, and by which alone, that can be satisfied. For this reason, no babe is born into a blank world, which he can later carve up to suit himself, or into a virginal world which he can make over to suit himself. A child is born into a world of farmers, teachers, masons, sailors, huntsmen, writers, doctors, clergymen, etc. Our world is a world of crafts. We did not make it that way. We did not design it to be that way. We had no choice about it. It is that way forever and by virtue of its nature, whether we like it or not. Therefore, there are in the world a number of great ways of work always going on by which we have food, housing, medicine, the arts, and so on forth — it is because this is true that we say that a man "enters work," or is "in work," or is "out of work."

The Masonic picture of a youth who stands erect on his own feet to face the Craft which he has chosen and who submits himself to it under a pledge which is the life-or-death principle, is, we Masons assert, a true and sound and complete picture of every youth in the world. For any boy to stay out of work is a certain road to ruin. For any boy to suppose he can enter work in general and no form of work in particular, and on his own terms, is folly because it is impossible. He was born to be a man, and just because he is a man, he must enter a craft. What Craft it is for his wisdom to decide, and he must train and educate himself.

CHAPTER XI
GREAT SYMBOLS

2nd Group
The Master — The Lights — The Level

5. ***The Master***. A youth came into the Craft of Freemasons at about twelve years of age and for seven years was under the guidance of an experienced Master until he could prove a firm understanding of the many arts of architecture. It called for toil, drudgery, studies, and obedience. Certainly, under those stern and exacting craftsmen, it must often have been even more painful than the labor itself. Then, his ability proven, and his character approved, he was declared to have been "made a Mason" and was raised to the status of Master.

Our Speculative Fraternity is erecting no buildings, nor can it keep a young man at work for seven years. It uses *the Mastership* symbolically. Its purpose is to establish in every Candidate's mind that the Operative Masons demanded the mastership as the indispensable qualification not because they were Masons but because they were serious workmen. They would have made the same demand if they had been weavers, smiths, carpenters, or cooks. For that very reason, the ritual means the same actual and literal training for mastery that the Operative Freemasons demanded.

From the standpoint of modern American customs in work and among workmen, there are two extraordinary facts about the system of apprenticeship and mastership. One is the fact that each man had to acquire mastership in the work of his craft, or he could not become a member of it or even earn wages. There were no exceptions to this law. The other is the fact that complete mastership was demanded. An apprentice was not permitted to learn one-third of the work, half of it, or three-fourths. There were no various grades of membership in the craft, with part of the membership doing the simplest work for the lowest pay, part doing the half-skilled work for half pay, and part doing the difficult work for the highest pay. There was no compromise. Either a man learned his work completely, or he was not permitted to work. Either he earned the same wages as his fellow craftsmen, or he earned no wages. Each workman was a master workman.

Such was the law of the crafts and guilds century after century. It was never a counsel of perfection or an unattainable ideal but an established rule so old that it went so far back that no man's memory ran to the contrary. And yet, to us, it seems incredible. We take it that a "master" is an exceptional man. He is the man pointed out and receives higher wages. He acts with bravura and is the "expert." His chief distinction in our eyes is that there are so few of him. As for other men, who are not "masters," they are "hands," "helpers," or "employees."

Can we go on with our system of the untrained, the half-trained, with non-masters? If the history of work can be trusted as our guide, we must answer that we cannot, for two reasons. One of the reasons is that using untrained or half-trained men is too expensive, and it necessarily must be so. While it is possible to cut any kind of work up into smaller and smaller pieces so that any one piece shall be simple enough for an untrained man to do it, you cannot cut the workmen's needs into smaller and smaller pieces. The wife and children of a man who makes one-ninth of a product must have as much clothing, as many pairs of shoes, food, and as much schooling as the family of the man who has mastered the whole of it. It is useless to argue that families can live on less and less because there is one minimum below which they cannot fall without falling into degradation — an absolute minimum below which they cannot fall without perishing. In the long run, over the whole nation and the generations, men must be masters at what they do to earn as much as they need. The other reason is that the world's work cannot be done except by masters. Half-hearted work is never like a set of steps where you can mount three or twelve steps and do one as easily as the other. It is like an organism in which you must have its whole or none. Mastery is the adequacy of the workman to his work as a whole. If he lacks that mastery, he falls out of the ranks of craftsmen and becomes a craftsman's mere helper or servant.

6. ***Light***. Any child in the second grade would insist that nothing could be more evident than the proposition that 2+2=4. They would demonstrate it on the spot and in an instant by holding up two fingers of one hand alongside two fingers on the other. They would be right about it. Nevertheless, when Russell and Whitehead came to write their *Principia Mathematica*, they had to fill more than 200 pages with sound reasoning about the nature of numbers and the axioms, postulates, rules, and presuppositions of

arithmetic before they were able to give a rigorous mathematical proof of the proposition that 2+2=4. Many of the truths which appear to be the simplest and most obvious are the ones in which lie the deepest and dizziest depths of thought. A Newly-Made Mason must keep this fact before him when he studies the symbols in the Ritual of the Three Degrees. Let him not deceive himself by what may appear to be their obviousness, simplicity, or smallness. There is not one of them which is not as old as time and as extensive as space. Each of them is such that when a student gains an understanding of it. The symbol tells him, "And now there is yet more in me; continue with your study." They are the proverbial "onion" with one layer after another.

The Operative Masons had a stern and strict law against working at night, but they sometimes had to work or assemble on a dark day or in a shadowed room. When they did, they used large tallow candles set in floor pedestals called Great Lights. They used hand candles called Lesser Lights when they needed illumination close up and on a small detail. It is interesting to note that the translator of the *Book of Genesis* must have had these candles in mind when he says that God created the Greater and Lesser Lights in heaven in the fourth chapter.

The symbolism of Light refers to these visible and material lights. In modern times, we could also use kerosene lamps or electric bulbs, or else it refers to actual and material daylight or moonlight. The ponderable lamps or candles, visible to the physical eyes, are not turned into something other than themselves. They were not changed into phantom, mystical, or ineffable illumination "never seen on land or sea," nor into metaphors.

In the lodge, the Candidate is bidden to observe the Lights and find Light. There would be no purpose in having them there if they were not to be used there. If a man is seeking some type of mystical light, some initiation into a remote or mystical art, he should go elsewhere to seek it. These particular Greater and Lesser Lights are in the Masonic lodge and are there for Masonic purposes. Craftsmen must have light to work. A builder cannot work unless he can see. He cannot use his hands unless he can use his eyes. He cannot see his material, understand how to work with it, or gain any knowledge of it unless he can get light on it. "Let there be light" is a motto, but it also is a direction because it means that the Apprentice must get his work into a good *light,* or he cannot do good work on it. He must be able to understand it. This recognition of the need for having *light* to work shows once and for all how absurdly mistaken the notion that Freemasonry is a secret society in the sense of being a hidden society. The rumor that Freemasons love the dark and conceal from view what they are doing or are employed in practices too mysterious to bear the light of day is nonsense! If true, how would these gossipers explain why a darkness-loving society chose "Let there be light" for their motto? Why it is that in the ritual, in some fifty different rites, ceremonies, emblems, and symbols have as their burden a man's need for lights, for more light, and enlightenment!

The Greater Lights and the Lesser Lights are nothing more than the light a Mason needs to do his work. Where is he to find that light? The answer is itself extraordinarily illuminating to any man's mind. He is to find it in the Greater Lights and the Lesser Lights. These are nothing but the Craft itself—the worldwide fraternity with its arts and law. In the language of words instead of symbols, the Apprentice is to find light in his work and for his work in his work. You learn the work by plunging into it. You gain knowledge of the work by doing the work. You study the ritual, philosophy, history, practices, rules, laws, etc. Each step you take throws light on the next step, the work is itself the enlightener of the workmen, and it is in work and not elsewhere that he learns to understand it. If this is true of the Masonic Craft, it is true of the apprentice in any other craft. He becomes enlightened as he becomes engaged in it, and each craft has its own Great Light.

7. ***The Level.*** Most of The Operative Freemasons were more religious than we Speculative Freemasons are, although we may talk more about it. Their work on stones, walls, and buildings with metal tools may appear more "materialistic" than our lodge work and, therefore, farther away from what we call "spiritual." But was it in reality? The *spiritual* in man is not the least material or the most remote from matter. It is that in a man using which he understands material things can work with them, use them, and master them for his purposes. If we could go into the history of the Operative Freemasons thoroughly enough to get into their skins, we may discover that they were deeply and sincerely religious because they did work with material things. They dealt daily with things no man could make, with mathematical laws, men did not enact. They were at grips with forces that no man could alter. They had to conform to the nature of things. They knew that the nature of things never alters itself to suit the desires of a man. They saw that men are all level and equal so far as the nature of things is concerned.

When, therefore, the lodge teaches the Candidate that he must meet his fellows "on the level," it is a lesson to reach deep within us. It is not an attempt to have him ignore the unavoidable differences among men in body, mind, ability, character, or personality with an amiable and sentimental lack of discrimination. The blurry and Utopian "leveling down," taught by the doctrine of equalitarianism, is not taught in the lodge. How could it be that members are in grades and officers have places and stations? The lodge's command that the Candidate is to step out on the level is no gesture of amiability. Rather it is a stern and ruthless order. If the Candidate is a young snob or a self-conceited egotist, it can be a painful ordeal because it does not imply that a Candidate is to step down to meet other men on the level but is to step up.

No exception will be made of you, Brother Candidate. You will never have it easier than other men. You may in the world outside be proud of your 'who,' but neither you nor any other 'who' makes any difference to the Master when he sets the Craft at work. When you lift the stone, it will be as heavy as when another lifts it. If a tower falls, it will crush you as quickly as any other. If you botch your work, it will be thrown on the rubbish heap as quickly, even though the Master is your father, or the Senior Warden is your uncle. Gravity is gravity for you, the same as for any other. A triangle is a triangle. Cold is cold, and rain is rain. The day's work is as hard. You have no business here unless you have the manhood to stay 'all-square' with your fellows, the fortitude to stand up with them, and the ability to come up 'level' with them."

CHAPTER XII
GREAT SYMBOLS

3rd Group
The Letter G — The Ashlars — Ruffians — Circumambulation — The Master

8. ***The letter G***. The "G" hangs on the wall above the Master's Station. It is one of the most important symbols that we have. Klein described it as the "one great symbol." It stands for geometry. Not for geometry in general, or the abstract, but geometry as used by Operative Freemasons. It is used as they learned and understood it in their centuries of work in building. Therefore, it is a Masonic symbol, and as we use it, it is wholly and exclusively ours. But the unqualified statement that it stands for geometry is not completely correct and must be amended to read "it

stands for geometry – as the geometry known and used in Freemasonry."

Freemasons learned in the earliest period of their history that geometry consists of the properties and attributes which belong to the physical world. "Wherever there is anything at all, matter is there." It is eternal because it belongs to the nature of things. However, the matter of Earth differs from man, plants, animals, or God. Matter has inertia. Matter has mass and weight, but it does not change without outside stimulus. It is not a living thing, at least, "living" as we understand the word. Still, there can nowhere be plants, animals, fish, or anything else unless something of matter is there. It is such that many material things are always coming into existence everywhere. These things differ greatly among themselves, but in each and all of them are some attributes or properties which they have in common. Everywhere among material things are self-same, invariable, and invariably to be expected. They are the attributes and properties not of this or that material thing but of matter itself.

It is at this point that we find geometry. Material things themselves, objects, or forces, or energies, or space, or time, etc. have in themselves, and not from being acted on from without, a way of breaking into planes (as crystals do), or of splitting along straight lines, or of falling into the shapes of globes and spheres (as rain does), or of moving in lines – curves, circles. They move at angles to each other or lie parallel to each other. They fall toward the earth vertically. In them are countless points, frames of reference, perpendiculars, etc. – thus, a single raindrop exhibits a whole geometry. It exists in a spherical drop, falls in a straight line, strikes the plane surface of a pool, sends out a ripple in the form of a circle, and falls along the lines of motion. The line is at right angles to the plane of the pool upon which it falls, and the drop itself is a point with a position in the frame of reference (the event as a whole).

The Operative Freemasons did not begin as abstract geometers working with definitions in the form of words and with diagrams to represent properties and attributes. They began as workmen in stone and erected structures of stone. They found the rules and principles of geometry for themselves as they went along and found them from the stones. Therefore, they began their geometry with the full knowledge that it consists of certain properties and attributes of matter. Since they operated in that manner, they never fell into the superstitious delusion many theologians and philosophers would fall into. The concept that matter is "materialistic," something sensuous, gross, or "low," or is somehow the foe of the spirit and the enemy of the mind was not the opinion of the Operatives. To them, matter had a meaning the exact opposite of "materialism." They found that by understanding matter's geometric attributes and properties, they could use and incorporate material things in everything spiritual, moral, social, and religious. They proved this in their cathedrals and churches, which were material structures and yet, for that very reason, were awesome, beautiful, and full of speech, instinct, and thought. In the words Matthew Arnold, they were "the friends and aiders of those who would live in the spirit." All these things which the Freemasons learned about matter, which are symbolized by the letter G, were true then, are true now, and will be true forever. There is neither need nor excuse for us to set up any opposition between matter and spirit, body and mind, science and religion, machinery and culture, or money and morals. We do not need to cut our national life into two opposing schisms: work, industry, and trade on the one side and religion, morality, and art on the other.

9. ***The Ashlars***. Ritualists of a century or a half ago fastened on the two Ashlars, *Imperfect* and *Perfect*. This was a misfortune because it misled our symbologists into writing many pages on the idea of perfection and many

times as many pages on the idea of a cube. Neither of these has any connection with the Ashlar symbolism. As we learn from many of the old Fabric Rolls, Ashlar was a Medieval builder's name for a stone. The symbolism represents the contrast between a stone on which no work had been done with the same stone on which work had been completed (one stone, not two, is denoted by the symbolism). In its state, before any work is done, it is not Imperfect, implying that work had been done on it but that the work had been faulty. A correct name would be Rough Ashlar or even Unworked Ashlar. When a stone was finished for use in a wall so that one surface, or two opposite surfaces, could be made flush with the face of the wall, it was called a *perpend ashlar* – perhaps some old writer or monitorial misread this word for "perfect." When a Candidate comes through the Inner Door at the beginning of the First Degree, he is a Rough Ashlar; at the end of the Third Degree, he is a finished product, ready for his place in the wall, which means he is ready for membership. His value for Freemasonry is measured by the amount of work done upon him during that period.

It may strike our ears as something harsh, or even as a piece of gaucherie in print, to liken a man to a stone or to say that work is done *on* him. But it is only the language that shocks us because if we consider the matter, we shall soon see that the idea has escaped our attention, not because it was too exceptional to see but too familiar to see. If we look for it, we can see it everywhere. Before he started school, a boy of six was a rough ashlar. By the time he graduates from school, he is a perpend ashlar. During those twelve intervening years, many teachers have worked with him. This work was done at a high cost to taxpayers, and unless that work has been botched or the boy had nothing in him, his monetary value (to the community and himself) is many times what it would have been had those teachers not worked upon him. How easy for them to fall into the way of speech where they instructively talk of "pounding it in," "driving it into him," or "nailing him down." It has been working for him and for them both. To school, to teach, to instruct, to train, to drill, to direct a man, to polish him, to coach him, to initiate him, to "tell" him, etc. – each and every one of those is a way of working on a man. Men cannot do work until work has been done on them. Economists estimate that it comprises one-third of the total amount of the work done by any nation and that men thus *worked* represent a full half of its wealth. And if none of this work on men were done, any nation would go bankrupt in a few years.

10. ***The Ruffians***. Every human on the planet sleeps and wakes until, one day, they will do so no more. We have no choice in the fact that our days on Earth are numbered. But in all other things in life, we have daily choices to make. Our choices may be simple ones having to do with our dress for the day or what we will eat for breakfast. The choices may also be life-changing decisions. If we see someone dropping an envelope of money, do we give it back to them or, do we steal it and enjoy the temporary benefits that a bit of extra money will give us. What we do and the choices we make affects us on a temporary physical basis and on a long-lasting ethical journey. The Legend of Hiram provides the Newly-Made Mason with rich philosophical and moral lessons from which he can find new value with each review.

At first examination, we can see that Hiram had a choice to make. He gave his word on a matter of importance, and three Ruffians demanded that he break his vow. They wanted him to give them what he promised not to give. They even threatened to take his life if he would not give them what they wanted. Hiram realized that we all live and die. We have no choice in that. But he also realized that *how* we live is very much our own choice. Hiram made the decision not to live his life without honor.

He refused to give them what they wanted. The ruffians made the decision to make good on their threat when they did not get what they wanted. This lesson is a study of morality and the value of life with and without honor. But it does not end there.

Like all symbolic lessons of value, a deeper examination of this lesson can provide us with more than is seen at first glance. Let's look deeper at this lesson. We live in sturdy wood and brick homes to protect us from the outside elements. At one time, communities built high walls around them to protect the citizens from outside invasion. Even to this day, most countries have armies to protect from those outside attacking them. But the Lesson of Hiram shows us that the danger is not always from the outside. This was an *inside job*. The Ruffians were workmen on the Temple. They were Freemasons! How could this happen?

No one knows the private thoughts, beliefs, or desires of another. The Legend of Hiram teaches us the dangers from within and from *our own* who have not properly learned our lessons. Freemasonry offers profound lessons of honor and integrity. We are taught to be peaceable members of society, to practice charity, and make every effort to improve ourselves daily. The legend of Hiram teaches us of the dangers and harm that can come from within our own ranks when we fail to teach or *weed out* the unworthy from our ranks. We are taught that sometimes the most important choices can be the most difficult.

11. ***Circumambulation***. From a position immediately within the Inner Door, a man is conducted on a symbolic journey, ultimately bringing him to his starting point. The name of this ceremonial progress is *Circumambulation*. But it is not used in its original or etymologic sense of walking about in a circle but rather in its looser sense of a journey outward, and about, and a return. This progress continues in an odd, stiff, almost mechanical manner as if it were a

robot moving, not a man. There are advances in straight lines, turnings at right angles, swerving about a pivot in a curve, and passing from one station to another. The words occasionally sound like voices out of the night and use unfamiliar phrases. Masons of countless number have commented on a feeling of something archaic, as if some rite or ceremony had wandered out of the Ancient World.

We Modern men are "smitten with the superstition of being busy." Above any generation before, we make a great clatter about our way of living because we no longer live on or next door to our place of work. We must spend enough time going to and from work to earn a second living. We are the busiest people who have ever lived, yet we many times give almost no thought to work itself. Where a hundred of us have clear ideas about sports, politics, religion, or entertainment, only few have ideas about work. The result is that we are not observant of the things belonging to work and fail to see what goes on under our eyes every day of the year. One of these things which we overlook is that every good workman has good form.

A man working in a machine shop must go from one machine to another. If he works in an office, he goes from one desk to another. If he is a farmer, he goes from his house to the barn and then to the fields. The instances in which men in any form of work must thus move or travel around are innumerable. When thus moving, they mostly walk in lines as straight as possible. They take turns at nearly a right angle and move in curves as near a circle's curve as possible. They do so for the same and apparent reason that no man is willing to waste a lot of useless steps, time, or energy. As said in this chapter, there is geometry in the nature of things. Form in work is nothing other than action per that geometry. Instead of these movements taken in Form (Circumambulation) being odd or archaic, they are the opposite. If, at work, a man went wandering about aimlessly, with no sense of direction, that would be seen as questionable, wasteful, and odd. We are taught to "move with a purpose."

This is also true of the movements, motions, and actions of the body, eyes, head, hands, feet — standing or sitting. It is also true with using tools, handling materials, looking, listening, turning, starting, and stopping. Awkwardness and ungainliness are nothing other than a man's failure to move himself according to the geometry in his own body. The famous masters of sports, baseball players, golfers, billiard players, riders, and swimmers, understand movement and the geometry of the body. Every movement of the athlete is valuable and considered. It is the hallmark of the expert. It is equally the hallmark of every form of work. Any master craftsman in any guild, art, or calling has smooth movement and a complete economy of effort. They do not wander about like an idling boy, flop about like a loafer, or blunder into things. We move with a purpose to reach a goal.

12. ***The Master of Masons.*** The Operative Freemason was untroubled in his mind on the subject of work. He knew that to be a man is to be a worker. Unless he quarreled with life, he did not quarrel with work — to hate, dread, or evade work was atheism. His feeling about it was religious in the true and universal sense of the word. Because he knew that while he was holding his tools in his hands, it was his own life that he was holding, as well as the lives of his wife and children. He did not quarrel with the *how* of work for the same reason. In the nature of things, there is one best way and only by which anything can be done. He accepted those ways, or hows (the knowledge of *how* is called understanding), as religiously as he accepted work itself. Therefore, if one of the commonest of these *hows* was for him to work in a body of men, he did not fight that fact. If in a body of men, a certain number are told when to begin, when to stop, and where to go, he gave no

thought to it because he knew that management, direction, and oversight are like work as much as sawing or hammering. He knew that these managers or superintendents were brother workmen, neither more nor less than other workmen. The function of management was in the spirit of work, not outside it.

If our world of work is shattered, if we are racked by "labor troubles," if we have strikes and panics, the fault is in this unspeakable folly about management over and above any other cause. On the other hand, we have fallen into the fundamental blunder of separating the functions of management and administration from work itself and the body of workmen in an attempt to make it something apart. A Master of Masons superintended a body of men who outranked any other men at the time in intelligence, skill, knowledge, and fame. A Master of Masons supervised a building far more difficult to construct and often as necessary and costly as any skyscraper in the new world. Yet he also was a working craftsman. He had been an apprentice for many years, had worked as one craftsman among others, worked for wages, and was under the same rules and regulations as others. He was not above, or outside, the body of men but was himself a member of it. But the great ambition of a modern master, superintendent, or manager often seems to be to get as far away from work as possible, to have the least possible hand in it. If the workmen organize themselves into associations and unions, the manager does not become a member but goes off with others of his ilk. A dichotomy, a schism, a chasm splits in two the world of work. It is no wonder these two unnatural divisions always conflict with each other.

Chapter XIII
Great Symbols

4th Group
The Search — Solomon's Temple — Clasped Hands

13. ***Search for that which was lost***. "Where is it?" When in the Third Degree, the Candidate searches for something lost, his quest is turned into an allegory. That allegory is a dramatization of the question mark. The asking of questions is not a science because questions can be asked about anything and everything. It is an art, or almost an art, because it requires much intelligence and skill to know the nature of the questions. We need to understand how to ask them and to know what kind of thing an answer is.

One of the supreme achievements of the 19th Century was a discovery made about asking questions by the French thinkers who founded mathematical logic. They discovered and demonstrated by mathematical methods that any question that cannot be answered is never a true question but necessarily a false one. By a false question, they meant any proposition in the form of a query that contains a self-contradiction or else is meaningless upon being analyzed. It may appear to be intelligent to a careless mind, and it may appear to have meaning and to be a genuine inquiry, but it never is and is only a string of meaningless words. This tricky and secret deceptiveness of the question which cannot be answered is almost always behind the scenes, hidden away inside it. Often the discovery of the trick comes explosively, and the discovery usually causes us to laugh. This fact is the key to the humor in *Alice in Wonderland,* in which everybody keeps asking questions, and half the time, they are false questions. When their falseness is shown up, the reader laughs. Why did Humpty Dumpty have to sit on the wall? Humpty Dumpty gave Alice answers, and he hoped they sounded very profound. Alice herself believed for a time in the mysterious fate which kept him on the wall. But the trick in it was Alice's assumption that he had to sit on the wall, whereas, as his fall demonstrated, he did not have to. Because her question presupposed something to be a fact that was not a fact, her's was a false question. Such a question cannot be answered because it makes an answer impossible.

A true question never proposes an unsolvable mystery, conceals a trick, or hides a self-contradiction. No sane man would try to ask an unanswerable question. If you ask me a question, it is a request for information that I possess and which you desire to have. You never ask a question because you do not expect to receive an answer. You always ask one because you *do* expect to receive an answer. If I ask you the day of the week, the time of day, or where Jones Street is located, it is because I believe you possess that information, and I would like you to give it to me. It may be that one cannot answer some question another asks him, but that does not prove that the question is unanswerable. Thus, if I ask you how to square a circle, I have not asked you a question because the words "square a circle" have no meaning. No sane man ever searches for something lost if, beforehand, he is convinced that it cannot be found. A Candidate would not search for a Word if no Word existed. If any man were to retort upon this that the word was too mystical or mysterious to be found, the reply would be that if there is any such thing, it is not a word.

The Allegory occurs within the Third Degree. It is enacted in the lodge. It occurs because of what went before it in the ritual, leading to something which follows it. Therefore, the Allegory is exclusively Masonic and must be interpreted in Masonic terms. Other allegories of a similar kind are used elsewhere, but this particular allegory occurs nowhere but, in a lodge, and is enacted by the Candidate. Its meanings are Masonic meanings.

There was once a Master of Masons. He was supervising work on the most famous building in the world. While other craftsmen had this or that part of the plan in their minds, the Master alone had the whole plan. This Master is lost, and the key to the whole plan is lost with him. The result is that the work comes to a stop. King Solomon comes to maintain order among the stricken craftsmen but does not have the plan. At this point, the ritual poses a question to the Candidate, which may be stated in our own words: "The Master is lost. What can we do? What can you do? Can you find him?" The Candidate's answer is to search for that which was lost. Did he find it? Yes, he discovered that he himself is the answer, for it is an Ancient Landmark of the Craft that no Apprentice is ever admitted into membership until he has mastered the art of Freemasonry, including the ability to occupy any Masonic office. If a veteran Craftsman drops out from old age, or a Master of Masons dies or otherwise passes on out of his office, a substitute is always at hand — "substitute" not meaning a makeshift but a replacement. What the Candidate discovers is that he is searching for his own mastership. Once he becomes Master of the Art, he can take any brother's place as Master of Masons. It was said that he was that which he found; he was the answer to his own question.

14. ***Solomon's Temple.*** The ritual is full of surprises — and surprise is one of the secrets of great ritualism. It rarely does what we expect it to do or says what we expect it to say. A member on the sidelines may grow drowsy in the middle of a degree if he has seen it a hundred times, but no Candidate ever does in a properly performed ritual. The Candidate never knows what is coming next. Solomon's Temple is a curiously interesting example of this element of surprise. It surprises us because we do not find it where

we expected to find it. Considering that it is the largest and most imposing symbolism in Freemasonry and so many things in the degrees refer to it or are described in terms of it, we naturally expect it to stand at the climax of the Third Degree, but it does not. The climax is in what happens to a man, not what happens to a building. The Temple stands in the center of the action in the Second Degree, not in the Third. Indeed, most of the action of the Second Degree occurs inside the Temple – in the Third Degree, it is merely a part of the background. There is a historical reason for this.

Until about 1740, lodges conferred only two degrees. The Making of a Mason was therefore completed in the Second, which had two names. A Candidate was made a full member of the Fraternity (a Fellow) in the Fellowcraft Degree. A Candidate was made a Master (a Master of the Art) in the Master Mason Degree. The new degree (it was new as an organized Rite, not in its content) should have been called the *Master of Masons Degree*. Calling it the *Master Mason Degree* has been confusing ever since. And it has been confusing because adding a Third Degree could not make over or revolutionize the old Two Degrees. Therefore, we still have the Sanctum Sanctorum in the Second. This Sanctum, the innermost recess of the Temple, means that a Candidate has mastered his goal. He has served his apprenticeship. He has learned his Arts and Sciences, and he cannot go further in the art because there is nowhere to go. The building which encloses this degree is an already completed one to represent the fact that he who was an Apprentice, has now mastered his art. He has completed the work of learning.

Another curious fact about Solomon's Temple is that it being Solomon's Temple has nothing to do with it. It could be Charlemagne's, Athelstan's, or any other building. In the Old Charges, it is not any building in particular. Also, and for like reason, it need not be a temple, though there are ritualistic advantages in having it one. As described in the Second Degree, it is evident that it is not the historical Solomon's Temple that is used, but the ritualist's temple. The Second Degree would be mistaken at almost every point if it were intended to represent the actual, historical Solomon's Temple. In reports of the actual Temple, the stairs were on the outside, not the inside. No one went into the Temple, still less into the Holy of Holies. There were no Greek Columns in it, no Three, Five, and Seven Steps, and no Rabbi ever delivered an 18th Century lecture on the arts, the sciences, and the orders of architecture. The ritualist is not a historian. He can play fast and loose with history, like the author of The Arabian Nights. Dates and places mean nothing to him. If he needs to have Euclid carry on a conversation with Solomon, he can do so; he is bound only by the rules of his art, not by the canons of history.

Solomon's Temple represents nothing occult, mystical, or mysterious. It is nothing more than a building, any building, any constructed piece of architecture. It is for that reason that it is of such paramount importance in our ritual. It is so charged with meaning not only for Masonic symbologists but also for Masonic historians. Maybe especially for historians because if a Masonic historian loses hold of that which Solomon's Temple represents, Masonic history will fall apart in his hands into a meaningless jumble. There are sound and apparent reasons for this, which are not far-fetched. They are equally true for any man, whether a Mason or not, because the reasons have universal validity.

Every art, calling, trade, profession, craft, or vocation has a changeless pattern, a fixed center, by which it is regulated, shaped, and controlled. Thus, the timber, the square, and the saw are at the center of the carpenter's world. At the center of the musician's world are notes, sound, and instruments. Symptoms, diagnoses, remedies, etc., are central to the physician's world. Any man in any art can go as far as he pleases and be as accessible as he desires, but he is harnessed to that which stands at the center. Therefore, he does references that center, and therefore his art has its own changeless and characteristic pattern. In Freemasonry, that controlling and regulating pattern has always been a building.

Freemasons have formed many associations, guilds, and city companies through the centuries. They have adopted a wide variety of rules and regulations. They have had many landmarks and have used hundreds of symbols. They work today in more than forty degrees. They have their lodges all over the earth. But everything they have been or have done has always, directly, or indirectly, been made necessary by building, or has referred back to the building, or belonged to the building art. Its pattern always has been the pattern of architecture. Even its nomenclature is an architectural one. Its philosophy of work, which has universal validity, and its own great contribution to the world, is set forth in the forms and terms of the builder's art. If this is an accurate account, then that which is meant by the symbolism of Solomon's Temple becomes a sovereign touchstone by which any Mason can detect Freemasonry's true and false interpretations. If the explanations are consistent with the pattern set by the art of architecture, they are true. If they contradict that pattern, they certainly are false.

15. ***Clasped Hands***. A chapter elsewhere on the Monitor states that the Monitor (or Exoteric Work) is not time immemorial or an Ancient Landmark. A group of English Masons produced it under the leadership of William Preston in the middle of the 18th Century. Preston was mistaken in his interpretation of the ritual at a number of points, and it was argued that Grand Lodges ought to prepare a new Monitor. The present instance is a case in point. In a clause in the Monitorial portion of the First Degree as used in some unwatchful Grand Jurisdictions, it

is stated that "our Ancient Brethren worshipped deity under the names of Fides, or Fidelity, which was sometimes represented by two right hands joined..." The statement is a catalog of blunders. Our Ancient Brethren did not worship Deity under any name except God. Pagans here and there worshipped Fides one or two thousand years before our Fraternity began, but even they did not worship Fides as a deity, but only as one of many small gods – no Operative was ever a pagan. Operative Freemasons did not use Fides even as a symbol, and it is doubtful if one in five thousand of them had ever heard of Fides – what had Medieval architects to do with ancient mythology? And who among the three to four million Masons in the United States has ever heard of the old Roman god or feels any need for a symbol of him? The Clasped Hands are exactly what they appear to be, two Freemasons grasping each other's hands.

When a veteran Operative Mason grasped the hand of a Newly-Made Mason, the two men faced each other, looked each other in the eye, and measured each other. If the veteran could have put into words what he put into his grip, they would have run somewhat as follows:

"In this work we work together, or we cannot work. If you fall down on your own work, you will render useless what I have worked on for a week or a month. If you miscalculate the stones in the arch the arch will fall, and the roof may fall with it. If it does fall, I as well as you may be under it. If you scamp your work on a wall, the wall may fall. If it does, it may fall on your fellows as well as yourself. The work we are doing here puts bread into the mouth of every craftsman, his wife, and his children. If you snarl it up, and bring it to a stop how can they eat? I have watched you as an apprentice and I now size you up as a man. With these things in mind, I am satisfied with you. I do not believe you will fail, fall, or back down. I accept you as a man upon whom I can rely as upon myself, and I give you my hand on it."

PART FOUR

CHAPTER XIV
RELIGION AND MASONRY

During the Middle Ages, Britain had two governments, side by side, equal in authority, the Civil Government with the King at its head and the Church with the Pope at its head. In the first instance, the Church governed itself and the religious Orders. But its rule also extended over everything outside the church, which in any way had to do with religion, directly or indirectly. These church rules sometimes were far removed from theology. For example, the Church prescribed how much money women could pay for their clothing, it could levy taxes, and had its own lawyers and law schools. The church had its courts, its trials, its police, and its penitentiaries – the word itself is a theological name, "place of penitence." Its rules were, in general, called *The Ordinances of Religion*. The body of its law was called *Canon Law*. This extended itself over Britain in the form of immovable rules which bore on almost anything a man could do. So large was this empire of the Church that at one period, it and the religious Orders together owned one-third of England. It had a larger revenue than the Civil Government. It even had its own army.

This religion called itself catholic, or universal, not only because it sought to extend itself over the earth to become the only religion in the world but also because it extended itself with an almost complete universality into men's daily affairs. It did not shut itself into one building or day of the week. There was nowhere a wall between the sacred and secular because the Church believed itself to have the authority to dictate to the secular at any desired point. It did not remain apart from politics, business, or work. Business contracts were drawn in theological language. Bankers were not permitted to charge interest because the Church condemned it as usury—one of the principal reasons for the poverty of the Middle Ages. Farmers planted, cultivated, and reaped according to a Church calendar and had special ceremonies for each work season. The crafts, arts, trades, and professions were organized in guilds, fraternities, companies, and sodalities. Wherever these touched upon any matter belonging to theology, faith, observance, or ceremony, they were regulated by the Ordinances of Religion. Their rules and regulations were drawn in the name of the Trinity and Virgin Mary. Apprentices were admitted by a religious oath. Each had one or more Patron Saints, observed the Saint's Day as a holy day, and went in procession to the Saints' Chapel. These holy days became so multiplied that as many as one-fourth to one-third of the days of the year were set aside for them – another reason for Medieval poverty.

The above facts explain a difficulty that for a long time puzzled many Speculative Masons. If Freemasons were all builders and architects in the literal sense for four or five centuries, and if the majority were operatives for two additional centuries, how does there come to be so much religiousness in the Fraternity? Why is its oldest document begun with an invocation to the Trinity and the Virgin Mary? Why an altar in the Lodge Room? Why a Volume of the Sacred Law? Why a religious oath? Why prayers? It is because, during the centuries of Operative Freemasonry, the Fraternity was as much under the Ordinances of Religion as other crafts and guilds.

The same facts also explain many elements of the ritual and the Ceremonies. They are there because, for centuries, the Ordinances of Religion required them to be there. Those Ordinances dominated men's thoughts, beliefs, conduct, clothing, marriage, death, customs, behavior, etiquette, and decorum. They made rules requiring painters to paint only pictures of certain kinds, even prescribed the colors used, and regulated sculptors in making statues. They censored speakers, meetings, writings, and studies. They allowed some arts and sciences and prohibited others. They made rules for how to walk, enter a room, what to wear, salutations, courtship, postures — nothing was too minute to be controlled. The consequence was that a man's life was filled with ceremonies, rites, and formalities, which was true for him even while he was at work. A number of those customs and ceremonies, as thus made compulsory over the centuries, continue in practice now. An example of compulsory customs is our having Patron Saints, which are, therefore, among the origins of our rituals and symbols.

When Masonic books began to be published in any number at about 1800 (and until professional Masonic historical scholarship became established at the end of that same Century), most writers faced a dilemma. They pictured the early Operative Freemasons as having been nothing more than stonemasons and day laborers. They believed that Speculative Freemasonry was almost akin to a religion, at the very least as a philosophy. They believed that there was much religious mysticism in it. How, then, could this Speculative Freemasonry have grown out of Operative? A number of writers cut this Gordian Knot by boldly bringing in an outside origin which was some form of religion or philosophy. They said this religion, or this philosophy, had settled itself into the old Craft, had taken it over, and produced Speculative Freemasonry.

It is impossible to accept such theories now after our scholarship has learned so much about Operative Freemasonry, which was not known in the 19th Century. For one thing, the problem no longer exists. The Operative Craft was filled with religiousness and religious or quasi-religious rites and ceremonies because of the Ordinances of Religion. Every other craft or guild was also filled with them for the same reason. Even the black-smiths had old traditions and legends about King Solomon, and the carpenters had legends about Jesus of Nazareth. For another thing, Freemasons never adopted any outside religion or secret cult, or philosophy for the same reason. The Ordinances of Religion made it impossible. If a Mason had taken up with astrology, alchemy, Kabbalism, or any other such esoteric faith or occultism, he would have been arrested, tortured, and burned at the stake. When Freemasons were at work on a cathedral, no priest (that we know of) sat in lodge with them; but Church rules dictated most of the details of carvings, sculpture, pictures, stained glass, altars, ambulatories, and chapels. It would have been impossible for the Freemasons to practice any secret cult inside their lodges without discovery or to have embodied its ideas or symbols in the buildings. Moreover, the Freemasons had no desire for heretical cults because they were Christian.

If this is true, how could the Freemasons originate something new, something undreamed of before, something startlingly unlike anything else thought or believed in the Middle Ages? Is it true? How and why did Freemasonry alone survive out of the many Medieval fraternities? And it not only survived but has grown and become worldwide! It is because the truths they found were not religious or theological, nor, as the word was understood in that period, philosophical. Freemasonry belonged to a different category and stood as far apart from religion or theology as mathematics does. This may be considered the most important of the many facts about Freemasonry and religion. Even in the period when the Fraternity was what we should now describe as very religious, it was not a religion. Its many religious ceremonies and observances were not peculiar to it but were the same as were enforced on every craft or fraternity by the Ordinances of Religion.

We Americans rarely see or participate in rites and ceremonies except in church. Therefore, we have fallen into the habit of thinking of ritual as a religious form in some sense or to some degree. A Medieval man could not have understood such an idea because he used rites and ceremonies daily. A farmer could not plow a field, cut his harvest, or slaughter the pig without due rites. A working man in shops and factories made a ceremony out of reporting to work in the morning. They saw in ritual no necessary connection with religion. What worth are rites when thus used so universally? Perhaps the most factual answer to that question was given by Confucius, certainly the most successful answer.

Confucius was unique among the founders of religions in that where the others told men what they must believe, he told them what they must do and refused to tell them what to believe. He did not create a new religion or theology, had students but neither disciples nor apostles, he did not even go about preaching or speaking. He wrote a few books, including *The Book of Poetry* (songs and music), *The Book of History*, and *The Book of Rites*. He did not even originate the larger part of the contents of these books but compiled them out of older writings. He didn't write them to become a Bible or, in any sense, a collection of sacred writings. They were to be used as texts by his students. Yet through their plain, simple, sincere pages, he became the teacher, exemplar, and shaper of the most populous community in the world for 2,500 years! What is even more remarkable in the eyes of us Westerners is that in his writings, that which did most to shape and guide some billions of men and women after him were the rites he recommended to his people. It is remarkable because we neither use rites nor believe much in their efficacy. What was Confucius' secret? He saw that there is a right way to do anything. You must find the right way to do something, and then do it the right way each and every time you do it!

There is a right way to greet a friend, enter a room, sit in a chair, eat at a table, address parents or children, etc. Through hundreds of other acts or occasions which recur continually. This "right way to do a thing" is the secret of our own ritual. When a Candidate is received at the Inner Door, when he takes his Obligation, when a Mason enters the lodge, when the Master opens the lodge, and so on through some 200 occasions or moments always, there is a right way to do it. And it is for that reason that it is done the same way each time. It is not to say that the Freemasons learned the secrets of ritual from Confucius. They most likely had never heard of him. Rather it is to say something to ourselves in order to cure ourselves of taking a ritual casually or of thinking of it more as a formality. The extraordinarily long history of Confucianism makes it impossible for any man to doubt the meaning or power of a true and sound ritual. And suppose any Mason has the impression that our ritual is a statement or teaching of religion. In that case, it is either because he has missed the weight and power of the ritual itself or because he has never examined it closely. It is neither a religious ritual nor a ritual of religion but is wholly and solely a craft ritual.

If what has been written is as well as completely understood, it gives in one stroke the connection between Freemasonry and religion — and that is that there is none. There is no more connection between Masonry and religion than between Masonry and science, education, politics, or language. It neither works for religion nor works against it. It began as a craft, and therefore the whole subject of religion was irrelevant to it. This is an obvious fact about the building craft because, in the nature of things, it is wholly separate and apart from theology. There can be no Roman Catholic geometry, Protestant engineering, or Mohammedan logic. It is equally true of modern Speculative Freemasonry because its Tenets, Landmarks, Brotherhood, Fraternalism, and Charity are self-same in every country and are nowhere altered by either religion or politics.

A Freemason in the year 1200 saw as clearly as we do today. Therefore, while he thought of himself as a Catholic, it did not occur to him to think of his art or craft as having anything to do with Catholicism. A man can have a religion, an art cannot. As long as Catholicism was the only religion he knew, as long as the civil and ecclesiastical laws compelled him to be a Catholic and threatened to hang him or burn him if he was not, he was a Catholic. After the Reformation had abolished those laws and had driven Catholicism out of the country, he was a member of the Church of England. By the time the first Grand Lodge was set up, he had begun to be free to belong to any church or denomination. But his being a Catholic, an Anglican, a Methodist, or whatever faith he chose, concerned him only in his private capacity as a man. He knew that it made no difference to his art of architecture or the fraternizing of men in the Craft because the Craft always has been non-theological. And now, with Freemasonry having become worldwide, he has larger liberty still, for he not only can belong to any denomination of his choice but can belong to any religion of his choice.

One of the most inexplicable facts in the many centuries of the history of Freemasonry was the Roman Catholic church's abrupt, unheralded, and unwarranted condemnation of it when in 1738, Pope Clement XII issued a Bull to excommunicate Masons. He condemned the Craft bitterly, as a few Popes have since, especially Leo XIII, who issued Bulls and Encyclicals against it. Clement XII was an Anti-Mason almost more than he was a Pope. Historians have not yet discovered why Clement acted in 1738, not even Roman Catholic historians, especially after his church and the Fraternity had been closely associated for centuries. He gave no sound reason because he had none. But he was old and almost senile and spoke with a most un-Christian bitterness. It is thought that he took the step because of a quarrel. Once he had taken the step, it was irrevocable, on the theory that the Pope is infallible, and the prohibition continues. It has accomplished no good purpose, and since the 18th Century, thousands of Masons were Catholics. In Ireland, there were so many that some lodges were composed wholly of priests. It is difficult to guess why they never discovered the Fraternity to be as evil, as atheistic, and as corrupt as Leo XIII declared it to be. If there was a quarrel, it was on one side only. Regular Grand Lodges do not exclude Catholics from membership. Consistent Catholics could not petition for membership after their Popes had forbidden it, but the prohibiting rules were Catholic and not Masonic.

The first of the charges of a Freemason, on page 50 of the first edition of the *Book of Constitutions*, makes this abundantly clear because it is the Constitutional law that both lodges and Masons must obey. It is entitled "Concerning God and Religion":

"A Mason is obliged, by his Tenure, to obey the moral Law, and if he rightly understands the Art, he will never be a stupid Atheist, nor an irreligious Libertine. But in Ancient Times, Masons were charged in every Country to be of the Religion of that Country or Nation, whatever it was. Yet it is now thought more expedient only to oblige them to that Religion in which all Men agree, leaving their particular opinions to themselves, that is, to be good Men and true, or Men of Honor and Honesty, by whatever Denominations or Persuasions they may be distinguished; whereby Masonry becomes the Center of Union, and the Means of conciliating true Friendship among Persons that must have remained at a perpetual Distance."

CHAPTER XV
PHILOSOPHY

Some six hundred years before the Birth of Christ, Greek thinkers and scientists made an important discovery. While there are countless separate, individual things such as plants, animals, and men, each one authentic, and no two identical, they nevertheless belong to a single, all-inclusive unity — to this, they gave the name *cosmos*. The Latins after them gave it the name *universe*. We use both words, and we also use the word *world*, but universe is mostly preferred. A century later, Socrates made a discovery almost as important when he found that although there are countless men, and each man has a mind of his own, the mind is everywhere and always the same thing. One man cannot use another's man's mind. Still, each and every man uses conceptions, knowledge, ideas, reasoning, and understanding whenever he uses his mind, and these activities are the same in every man. This discovery by Socrates gave thinking men the best hope they had ever had of being able to think or think out the cosmos. No man can know or comprehend the cosmos alone because he cannot think hard enough or live long enough. But if thinking and knowing are the same everywhere, then humanity can hope to know and understand the world because there are billions of men to think, and they have all the time to do it.

Early Greek thinkers devoted themselves to thinking about the cosmos and did so by attempting to answer the question, "How was the cosmos made?" This question inevitably broke into many questions: When did it begin? Of what is it made? Who or what made it? Or is it eternal? How was it done? There have never been more thinkers of the highest ability than the Greeks who labored to answer those questions. In their collective attempt to find the answer to that question, Pythagoras gave the name of philosophy. The philosophers were as cautious and ingrained in their thinking, systematic, and careful not to wander away from known facts as mathematicians. Their thinking, therefore, took the form of systems, hence the phrase "systems of philosophy." Many men, generation after generation, could work together in or for the same system.

One system was named and distinguished from the others by the general idea that it is used to describe and explain the cosmos. If a system attempted to explain the cosmos by the idea of matter, it was called a materialistic philosophy. If it used the idea of life, it was called a natural philosophy. There were many general ideas thus used: mind, atoms, cause and effect, change, progress, time, etc. The system founded by Democritus and of which Epicurus and Lucretius became champions attempted to explain the cosmos by the idea of atoms. Plato believed that the mind is the largest and most inclusive of things, so he explained everything in terms of it. Aristotle used a different method, but, in the end, he agreed closely with Plato. From their time until now, more thinkers have accepted their system than any other. Thus far, the United States has produced one new system, called Pragmatism, established by William James and John Dewey, which attempts to explain or describe the cosmos in terms of the idea of practice, experience, or doing.

The founders of early Christianity were theologians, but many had a philosophy and theology. Among those who did, the majority followed Plato, though many preferred Aristotle. After the time of Constantine, the Church set out to destroy non-Christian philosophy, science, mathematics, art, and literature. They spared neither of these Greek philosophers and ordered every copy of their books to be burned. They even abolished the old university at Athens, which Plato had established centuries before.

But in the meantime, many copies of those books had been carried down into Turkey, Syria, Iran, and Arabia, where they were translated into texts for use in schools. Of the two Greek philosophers, the Arabs preferred Aristotle. When in their conquests of the Near East, Egypt, North Africa, and Spain, they set up schools and universities in one city after another, Aristotle was always ranked first among their texts and teachers. Averrhoes and Avicenna, the greatest of their scholars and thinkers, were both Aristotelians.

Across southern Spain, the Mohammedans (called Moors) developed a remarkably high civilization, with cities of dream-like beauty, great literature, and many of the best schools and universities the world had ever known. Europe at that time was a cultural vacuum, which had no civilization, roads, cities, schools (or almost none). Ignorance and illiteracy were preached as religious virtues. They did not even have medicine, but in their dark, earth-floored huts depended on witchcraft. The result was that more and more of Europe began to look to Spain for knowledge, science, art, and education. More than one Pope called in Mohammedan (or Spanish Jewish) physicians, and there came a time when it began to appear that Mohammedans thought their theology and armies might conquer Europe as they had conquered North Africa.

When this danger was most critical, the Church was blessed with three champions whose fame, even after seven centuries, has not yet begun to diminish. These were Albertus Magnus, Thomas Aquinas, and Abelard. The three were worth thirty armies, and their work confined the Moors to Spain and prevented their spread across France, Italy, the Lowlands, and Britain.

It is impossible to describe or explain their work in one paragraph. It would be difficult to explain it to an American, even in many volumes, because it is so remote from our language and ways of thought. However, it is not impossible to see its general purpose or point. Aristotle's name had come to stand among Mohammedan peoples for medicine, mathematics, zoology, astronomy, architecture, and philosophy. The Christian Church had condemned Aristotle, and for all he stood. But unless Europe could have the arts and sciences (medicine especially), true Christianity would be destroyed, and when it was gone, Mohammedanism would move in.

What the three Christian champions did (and Thomas Aquinas principally) was to find a way to reconcile Christian theology on the one hand with Aristotle on the other and to do it without destroying either. And they also (what was equally necessary) to persuade the Pope to accept that reconciliation. The new system they developed was so large and complex that no one name could characterize it. But since it was worked out, taught, and completed in theological schools, it was called "schoolism" or Scholasticism. It was officially adopted as its only authorized philosophy by the Roman Church. A member of that Church was thereby officially committed by his vows of faith to accept the theological doctrines promulgated by St. Augustine, the Church's official theologian, and the philosophical doctrines of Aristotle.

The Operative Freemasons of the Middle Ages were closer to the Church than any other body of men not in monasteries or the priesthood because they were the Church's builders. A modern American builder can erect a church for any denomination using manufactured materials and works from blueprints. The Medieval Freemason processed his materials, supervised them, planned his work, and made the designs and models for each part. These were designs created especially for the building, not copied from books. To work under such conditions, he had to be in continual association with the churchmen he was working with. And since his decorations and carvings had to portray the teachings and doctrines of the church, he could do so only by having a thorough knowledge of church doctrines and practices. He had to put into stone and into the form of a building a whole system of ideas in which philosophy and theology were combined.

This philosophy was Scholasticism. Wherever the Mason went, he was surrounded by and saturated with Scholasticism. It was his mind's world. To define the Gothic Style as Scholasticism in the form of architecture would not be an adequate definition. The Freemasons and not the Scholastic philosophers invented the style. But even when the Freemason worked on castles, palaces, or other private or public buildings, he did not escape Scholasticism because it permeated everything. It shaped the British and European minds for three hundred years.

When we turn to the records of the early Operative Freemasons to find what their work was and what they did in their lodges, when we analyze the Rules and Regulations and the Old Charges and read the oldest lodge Minutes or histories, we find nowhere any trace of the Scholastic philosophy. No Assembly or lodge stated, adopted, endorsed, championed, or approved any other philosophy. When a historian asked the Operative Fraternity its philosophy, silence was returned. It had no philosophy, preferred no one system to any other, and it did not because the Freemasons could not see that either their Craft or their work was concerned with any system of philosophy, one way or another.

When the control, or the part control, of the lodges by Operative Masons, gave way after the Grand Lodge System was established and the Fraternity became wholly Speculative, there was no Scholasticism left in England except in the Roman Catholic Church, in Oxford University and a few small circles. Copernicus, Galileo, Francis Bacon, Newton, and Christopher Columbus, among others, each in his way, had battered it to pieces. They made it impossible for free and competent minds to believe in it.

But when the Mother Grand Lodge began to warrant its lodges here and there across the counties of England, it was surrounded as closely by a system of philosophy as Scholasticism had surrounded the Operative Lodges. The country had a philosophy of its own; here and there, an occasional school, circle, or thinker might have a different philosophy. But with these exceptions, England had but one philosophy. Englishmen thought out many of their questions in terms of religion, government, morality, and business in terms of it. Historians have called it British Philosophy; professional philosophers call it British Empiricism. John Locke (who probably was a Mason) was to it what Aquinas had been to Scholasticism. Isaac Newton was believed to be the greatest scientist in history because the English believed (and not without reason) that his science had proved Empiricism to be true. The governing idea of this philosophy was experience. The gist was to trust your senses, learn from experience, see how things work out, experiment, try this, and abide by the results. Whatever works out best is the truest. When turned upside down and translated into the terms of ignorance, it takes the form of a "muddle through."

The Speculative Fraternity had its birth and its first growth amid this ubiquitous Empiricism. Yet nowhere in the revised *Rules and Regulations*, the *Book of Constitutions*, any of the charters, or anywhere in the reorganized ritual is that philosophy so much as even mentioned. No Petitioner is asked to be an Empiricist; the Monitor contains no lectures on it. This is also true of the earliest lodges in the United States. American Colonists in the 18th Century were as saturated with the ideas of Empiricism as was the homeland (Franklin was the prophet here). John Locke's fame here was as great as at home, but for all that, no reference to that system of philosophy was ever made in lodge or Grand Lodge histories and Minutes or in Grand Lodge Constitutions.

These aspects of Medieval Operative Freemasonry and early Speculative Freemasonry are historical facts, not theories. Therefore, they are decisive, and since they are, a Mason can state without fear of contradiction that at no point in its history has the Fraternity adopted, endorsed, or championed any one system of philosophy. If ever it had done so, it is almost certain that it would have (for historical reasons) given its endorsements to one or more of the systems of philosophy named after Plato, Aristotle, Thomas Aquinas, or John Locke. But no Mason or non-Mason has grounds for saying that Freemasonry ever has favored any one system of philosophy or exhibited any interest in the subject of philosophy. The Landmarks would indeed be inconsistent with a certain number of philosophies. Still, if so, it is for a Candidate to decide whether his philosophy (if he has one) is one of them, for in the degrees, he is submitted to no philosophic inquisition.

The systems of philosophy differ much among themselves. They differ so much that more than one-half of the interest in the subject comes from the clash of one with another. Not even a Greek sophist could find much in common between the idealism of Bishop Berkeley and the materialism of Professor Haeckel or between the Scholasticism of Thomas Aquinas and the evolutionism of Charles Darwin. Nevertheless, all the systems of philosophy must necessarily use a certain number of ideas, just as men in the many branches of mathematics must use natural numbers. These ideas belong not to philosophy but are necessary for any thinking. Therefore, every man must use them whenever he thinks and no matter what he thinks about. Among these are such ideas as truth, reality, goodness, cause and effect, time, space, reasoning, life, matter, etc. They belong to the mind, not to the philosopher's mind, but to any man's mind, to the mind itself. Since this is true, anyone has on hand the materials out of which they can make a system of philosophy if they so desire. And many do; it is always a mistake to suppose that the only philosophers are professional. There is not a town of one thousand population in the United States that does not have at least one in it with a coherent, organized philosophy of their own and fifty who have thought much about philosophical subjects.

There may therefore be such a man with an organized philosophy of his own. He is neither a professor nor an author, delivers no lectures, and does not argue about it. He has not formed it idly, nor is it a plaything of his mind. It contains principles according to which he shapes the conduct of his life. Such a man is as free as anyone to petition for the degrees of Freemasonry. It may be that his philosophy is consistent with the Landmarks of the Fraternity. It may be that it conflicts with them; it is for him to discover the fact for himself, and the lodge trusts him to have the honor and truthfulness to do it. If he finds that his philosophy is in accord with the Landmarks, and if he is made a Mason, he will enjoy Masonry all the more for being a philosopher. While Freemasonry is not a philosophy, it has a number of those fundamental ideas in which philosophers have always been interested. It has that sweep of thought and that vast scope in which a philosopher feels at home. There is as much in Freemasonry for the mind as there is for the hands and the heart.

CHAPTER XVI
MASONIC RELIEF

When a man is at work, he uses himself, including his body, to make or produce something necessary to him and his family to survive. While he works, he works with (among many other things) machines, tools, electricity, chemicals, weights, and water. And almost any of these may be dangerous to him under some circumstances. Every occupation has its occupational hazards, and many men will become occupational casualties even with safeguards.

When any enterprise is set up and organized in any field of work, it must expect these casualties, and, in its plans and organizations, it ought to provide for them, their care, and remedy. The cost of that care and remedy should be included in the total amount of money that particular enterprise will cost the nation. And it does not matter what that enterprise's nature may be if men and women must work in it. It may be housekeeping, farming, practicing medicine, writing books, coal mining, preaching, railroading, and on and on. There will be casualties in any occupation. Most of them will be unavoidable, and their care and remedies will cost money. The amount of that money, along with provisions for the cure and therapy, ought to be a part of the organization of the enterprise, and the cost of them, to repeat, ought to be included in that enterprise's total (and social) cost. These inevitable casualties, with their remedy and care, is what is meant by relief. Therefore, this relief is an Ancient Landmark in any form or field of work and in any possible enterprise that may be organized. Therefore, it belongs to what work is; and any definition of work must include relief because work cannot go on unless relief is provided for. It will thus be seen at a glance that relief belongs to a category of things, unlike other categories with which we, in our carelessness of thought and speech, have so often confused it.

If a man refuses to work, he falls into poverty, and he and his dependents will starve unless the community's organized charities feed them, or he is sent to a workhouse where he is fed at the expense of tax-payers. There is nothing in common between his "case" and that of a locomotive engineer, who, at work and in the prime of life, is suddenly made a helpless cripple for the rest of his years by a wreck for which he was not responsible. To call the care given to him and the care given to the pauper by the same name charity is a vile perversion of language. If a man has in his character a normal amount of what we call goodness and if, in consequence, he is always willing to give out of himself something another wants, he is said to be benevolent, and his acts are acts of benevolence. If a man of means pays for, or endows, a hospital, library, church, park, or museum and does it out of love for his neighborhood or his community, he is a philanthropist — a word that defines itself since it is composed of two Greek words meaning "a friend" and "man." He is a friend of man. Only a barbarian or a savage could question charity, benevolence, or philanthropy. They are not being questioned here, either individually or by implication. Still, it must be evident that none of them is even remotely similar in its occasion, purpose, means, or spirit to relief. Relief belongs to the world of work necessarily and forever, in the sense that tools do, materials are used, or wages are paid. No enterprise could be set up with the expectation of employing workmen, and they could never organize themselves in a body to work together unless they included relief in their plans or their organization.

If the need for relief is inherent, like work, the cost of the care and remedy will be assessed against the total cost. It is this fact that many men find difficult to grasp or to understand, though it appears to be sufficiently obvious.

If, when coal miners are at work, the roof caves in on them, and one of them must be sent to the hospital for six months, it surely is plain that such a man is not in the same case as another man who lies in the same hospital from having driven an automobile while drunk. If you work in mines through your adult years, you have only one chance in twenty of not being hurt at least once. The danger of being hurt is inherent in mining, and since it is, the cost and responsibility for that danger belong not to the miners but to mining. Farming is almost as dangerous as mining; lumbering is equally dangerous; being a soldier or a sailor in war is far more dangerous. Men in many arts and professions have non-hazardous work yet run the risk of contagious diseases because they work with crowds or the sick and the diseased. Even the most sedentary occupations, such as scholarship, research, and writing, are hazardous because they are so wearing on the eyes, brains, and nerves. When the Ancient Greeks linked poetry and madness, they did not miss the mark, even medically, because the rate of insanity and suicide among poets has always been exceptionally high. No one has ever yet discovered a form of work without its own hazards, and those hazards always go along with it and belong to it as water always goes along with the work of a sailor. Freemasonry has known this fact for at least eight centuries. In the first lodge formed by the first Freemasons, relief was one of the rules organized in it.

"The Three Principal Tenets" is a phrase that carries in it no charge of excitement. It is a flat, inert, almost lifeless phrase with the somewhat pompous atmosphere of the English language as Samuel Johnson and his contemporaries used it. It is not even impossible that Samuel Johnson helped to author it because William Preston gave it its Masonic currency. Preston and Johnson were friends, and Johnson was very probably (though not certainly) a Mason. Masonic historians ignore the phrase,

Masonic essayists have discovered it with reluctance. Masonic poets have not sung about it, even the great mass of literature on the ritual has little to say about it. The words in it belong to that type of vocabulary that Johnson himself described as "soporific" because they put a reader or a listener to sleep. (The Standard Monitor has too much of this soporific vocabulary.) But none of this is as it should be "the Three Principal Tenets" are not archaic, thin, or soporific, and any Mason can find this true for himself if he digs into them. "Principal" means what comes first, which is most urgent, necessary, or must be done before other things can be done. The "Three" implies that while among the tenets, three are thus at the front and are most urgent, there are other tenets. There are possibly as many as forty tenets distinguishable in the ritual. It is significant to see that Relief is numbered among the three!

"Tenet" is a curious word, and to an etymologist is an exciting word partly because its history winds in and out and back and forth and is hard to trace. It is doubtful if even Sherlock Holmes could trace it through all its ramifications, partly because, in the word itself, something is exciting and dramatic. Ten was an Anglo-Saxon name for the number, found by adding one to nine. But this Anglo-Saxon ten may return to an old Sanskrit word meaning the ten fingers on the two hands. It is even more probable that the Latins made up their word *teneo* from an original meaning, the ten fingers, because *teneo* means grasping tightly with both hands, holding on for dear life, and refusing to let go. It still carries that meaning, or a ghost of it, in our *tenacious tenant* (who has a "hold" or possession of property; *freehold* is an Anglo-Saxon form), *tenement* (the property on which a tenant has a "hold"), *tenon* (from the French form of *teneo*), *tenor* (a man who can hold his voice at a pitch), *tenure* as the direction to hold to, etc., etc. Of these many forms of *teneo* our *tenet* is by far the most interesting because it carries in it a graphic idea: a tenet is a teaching, doctrine, or principle that a man takes hold of with (as it were) both hands. He holds on through thick and thin, which he clings to with tenacity ("glued to it"), which he will not let go until the last gasp, and at any cost to himself. Instead of the thin and lifeless word that we, in our casualness or indifference, have so often taken it to be, it is, in reality, a very masculine, exciting word. It is, therefore, to repeat significance to find that Relief is a Principal Tenet. If any reader should object to this, if an exaggeration has been committed according to his taste, let him read the history of Freemasonry. Relief was a Tenet in the first lodge, a principal tenet, and though during the centuries since that first lodge, the Fraternity has weathered many changes, been through the wars, and been battered without and within, it still keeps a fast hold on Relief — not once has it ever let it go. If it is not a Tenet in the historical and full sense of that word, nothing is. Operative Masons kept a grasp on it with both hands; Speculative Masons kept the same grasp. Freemasons always will because if the Fraternity were to let go of it, Freemasonry would cease.

Since the Operative Freemasons incorporated the tenets of our Craft, Operative and otherwise, there is no need for any Masonic student to look far to discover why Relief was one of them. Operative Freemasonry was as hazardous as mining, and lumbering are now, perhaps more so. The craftsmen worked with stones weighing fifty pounds to three or four tons. They had none of our modern heavy machines for hauling, lifting, or placing them. Their elevators, ladders, and scaffolds were wood. Their tools were of a shape to bruise or cut and were made of heavy metal. There were always the hazards that ensue from working on heights, with men above and below and about, where if a tool, or a stone, or a piece of timber slipped from a hand or broke off or fell, every workman in range was under risk of being struck by it. Along with these immediate and manual risks came the hazards of working in the open, where a sudden rain could blind a man's eyes, the snow could make a plank slippery, or cold could numb the fingers, etc. Of the 1,500 cathedrals erected, scarcely one failed to pay its tax in blood, and more than one Craftsman was buried under the pavement of a church he had helped to erect. Since almost the only safety device they had to use consisted of the men's caution, knowledge, and skill, we can understand why they swore in an Apprentice to obey and keep the rules and not be careless with an oath of an almost fierce earnestness.

But this was not the end of their hazards — not in the Middle Ages when the average life span was only twenty-two or twenty-three years. The Freemasons lived, most of them, in small villages or else were crowded together in narrow quarters inside a walled town. There was almost no surgery and little medicine. Midwives delivered babies. Against contagion, they had no protection, and when a plague or an epidemic arrived, they, like everybody else, were helpless. Fires, the chronic calamity of the Middle Ages with their towns full of wooden buildings, were almost as much dreaded as epidemics and more numerous. Under such circumstances, what would you do? What the Freemasons did was to organize themselves, with their families included, into a single, solid Community, and this Community made itself responsible for the unavoidable misfortunes of its members. As for the avoidable misfortunes, the drunkard, the idler, the criminal, and other such ilk, they dealt with them as an act of surgery; they expelled them. Relief, one of their Principal Tenets, and as a principal then as now, was exactly as described at the beginning of this chapter, the care and remedy for the casualties in the world of work. Any one of them, as a man or a woman, could be as charitable, benevolent, and philanthropic as he desired. But it was Relief which was the law of the Craft, and every Mason contributed his share to it in the same way, and for a like reason, that he had to contribute his share of the work.

When the ancient Operative Craft was put to new Speculative uses, the old law of Relief did not alter an iota, except that it was made to apply to members in any other craft or any other form of work. The members of our Speculative Lodges may choose, individually or collectively, when and as they desire, to give their money or time to charity, benevolence, or philanthropy. But on the question of Relief, they have no choice. It is a Landmark, a Tenet; it is not a matter of "if" it is the law. The money spent by a lodge for Relief is like the money spent for the sake of any of the other Masonic Purposes. It is part of the cost of operating the lodge, and it, therefore, is included in the dues, which are each member's equal share in those expenses.

CHAPTER XVII
MASONIC ETIQUETTE

Almost always, when we come to any of the large themes in Freemasonry, we can find the shortest path to the heart of its meaning by philology, especially by its department of etymology, the origin, and the history of words. With only a few exceptions, the name of any subject is that form of word called a *term,* and if so, the origin, history, and meaning of the term is a true definition of the subject. But in this case of etiquette, philology plays us false; it even tells us a lie, and it is doubtful if any other subject in the world has been more arrogantly misnamed. As the sound suggests, it is a French word meaning "according to the card." It is supposed to have originated in the custom in high society of handing each guest at a reception a card to show him his place in the order of precedence according to rank. It has ever since borne about with it the stilted air of the drawing room and looks, as the

Duchess said, "like something made by Watteau." Certainly, it is on the "satin side" of things, and snobs will not admit that any man or woman not in high society should be permitted its use. Nor do the guidebooks to its mysteries help us with the notion that etiquette is a matter of correct manipulations of teacups and the graceful choice of forks. It is all very strange. The theory that a few 17th Century Frenchmen invented it and then propagated it over the world is the kind of miracle that history refused to accommodate within its pages. It is especially so because the greatest master of etiquette the world has ever seen lived twenty-two hundred years before the 17th Century.

A calculus of population has estimated that during the twenty-five centuries since he lived, Confucius has been the exemplar, model, guide, and teacher of some ten billion men and women. This is remarkable in itself. It is more remarkable that he did not invent a new religion or compose an original book. It is still more remarkable because what Confucius gave Asia was etiquette. Confucianism may be defined as High Etiquette – as Etiquette *sub specie aeternitatis* (of an eternal kind). But Confucius would have scorned the childish fancy that etiquette could be so trifling as a set of cards to ensure that a waspish old duchess did not move toward the dining room ahead of a waspy old princess. "What," he would have exclaimed, "has that to do with it! Etiquette," he would have said, with all his great gravity and sincerity, "is eternal."

As a young man, Confucius put in years of drudgery to master a number of books on rites and ceremonies that were already ancient in his time. These books were arranged around the idea that there are a number of special and ceremonial occasions in which every well-bred man would participate. These books gave the forms, words, and music for these ceremonial occasions. Confucius first proved his great originality of mind by going beyond this scheme of special and ceremonial occasions to see that many occasions arise for everyone. They arise not out of accidental circumstances but of the nature of man and the world. Typical of these (there are hundreds of them) are such occasions as meeting an acquaintance on the street, entering the door of a friend's home, being a guest at a table, taking part in a conversation, sitting and rising, dressing to suit an occasion, salutations, visiting the ill, meeting the elderly, meeting a youth, etc., etc. Seeing this is true, he passed far beyond the formal and the artificial and the arbitrary and entered that which is eternal.

His next stride forward and, in yet greater originality and eagerness, was his seeing that there is always one right way to do these things! On each occasion, the manner has much, or everything, to do with how we do things. Unless a man does things correctly, he does not do them at all. That, to him, was the substance of etiquette. People and countries, languages, costumes, food, and native idioms differ, but it does not matter. The right way of doing a thing is the right way and the only way under any or all circumstances. Therefore, etiquette is universal and everlasting.

Until well into the 19th Century, it was easy to believe that etiquette was a local and more or less modern art, as the name implies. People believed it was practiced in its perfection in France and with somewhat less perfection in Italy and Spain. The French even admitted that the British had a little of it though the British would not admit that we Americans had any of it. Then as more and more men began to travel, as more and more went to live around the world, and still more after anthropologists began to understand peoples in those distant (from Europe) countries, it was discovered that Confucius had had the truth of the matter all those centuries; every society has etiquette.

And wherever it is, it is accurate. It is never a measured hypocrisy nor a piece of theatrical make-believe. Nor is it done for show. On the contrary, any given detail in etiquette will stand the same test for its reality as anything in mechanics and the same tests for practicality as anything in business. There is no need to offer one proof after another of these statements because one proof is, in principle, the same as any other. What are good manners at the table? To eat food in the way that is called for by the food itself. Coffee is enjoyed from the cup instead of the saucer because it spills too quickly. Bread is handled with the fingers because it is dry and needs to be broken. Meat is stabbed with a fork because it slides off a knife. But a knife is used for butter because it must be spread, and so on and forth. If you and I are acquaintances, why do we pause, shake hands, and speak if we meet on the street? This salutation allows having something to say on such an occasion because it belongs to acquaintanceship. If I step on your foot in a crowd, I say, "Excuse me," to show that it was unintentional. Why give older people the right of way? Because it is difficult for them to move quickly. Why "ladies first"? Because that which comes second is almost always something for a man to do. Why wear party clothes to a party? For the same reason that a man wears a business suit to his office or overalls to his shop. Clothes are selected and designed for the use to which they will be put. And so, would the long catechism continue. There would be nowhere in it any least detail genuinely belonging to etiquette which would not have an equally pragmatic sanction.

Once etiquette is understood, Masonic Etiquette is readily understood because it is in the lodge what it is everywhere else. There is no such thing as *Masonic Etiquette* in the sense that Masons have manners peculiar to themselves. It is Masonic only in the sense that it is the point of circumstances and occasions that are not found outside a lodge. The Work of the lodge has a large number (about 200) of separate occasions, events, actions, or ceremonies in which the manner of doing them is either all-important or is largely so. In each instance, there is a right way to do it. That right way is etiquette. That etiquette is, therefore, not determined arbitrarily or according to the modes and fashions of the time. It is not for show or ostentation but belongs to the nature of that which is done. A member, visitor, or Candidate knocks at the door. Instead of hurrying to a seat, he "advances," possibly with an escort, and then he salutes. If he is a member, he cannot take the floor during discussion unless he stands, salutes, and does not speak until he receives recognition from the East. Officers wear insignia and regalia and have titles to identify them as Officers wherever they are.

A Master could not preside over a lodge without having the whole lodge in view. Therefore, nobody sits, stands, or moves between him and the Altar. In a procession, there is an order of precedence. Once a procession arrives at where it is going (a room, a table, etc.), the Officers will have places and stations of their own. Therefore, an order of precedence prevents confusion. If a Grand Master enters and is received with Grand Honors and is escorted to the East, where he assumes the gavel, the form of reception has an official meaning because it signifies that he is there in his official capacity. But if he salutes at the Altar and then sits on the sidelines, it signifies that he is there not in his capacity as Grand Master but as a member or visitor. The whole system of Etiquette, for individual Masons, for lodges, and Grand Lodges, is at every point real, actual, necessary, official, and is for practical purposes. Any lodge member who doubts the full proof of this statement can prove it to their satisfaction in the Landmarks, Constitutions, general laws, rules, and regulations, which at many places provide that a willful violation of Etiquette is un-Masonic conduct. The guilty member may be penalized by reprimand, suspension, or expulsion.

Outside the Lodge Room, men divide themselves into sets, classes, and distinctions which no one of us can override, however great may be his equalitarian passion. Roman Catholics and Protestants, Jews, and Gentiles, rich and the not-rich, Republicans and Democrats, etc., but etiquette equalizes these differences inside the Lodge Room. The men present speak the same idiom and move in a common measure. Before he sits down to preside over his lodge, the Worshipful Master has assurance that "on this side of the Tiler," events and occasions will march beautifully. He will need no self-sacrificing patience to "suffer fools gladly" because no fools will suffer. He will sit pleasantly through the hour because his office is itself a guarantee of peace and harmony. There is an Etiquette for himself and his members, which insures him and them against complications and embarrassment.

The name of the first Duke of Marlborough (one of Winston Churchill's remote ancestors) is classical in military history, not for his genius in one campaign but for his consummate ability on any field in any war. But the one victory which everlastingly confirmed his high standing among generals was his command at the Battle of Malplaquet on September 11, 1709. With his army of British, Dutch, and German soldiers, he defeated France in one of the last of the countless wars between France and Britain. By common agreement among military authorities then and since, it was one of the most brilliant battles in history. Under any other circumstance, British men and women in Britain and America would have celebrated that victory with a week of fetes and bonfires, burning every night from hill to hill. But the victory passed almost unnoticed, stirred not a pulse, and even when the war ended, Marlborough himself was nonplussed by the unwarming welcome with which the people greeted his return. The reason for that indifference lay in one of the most extraordinary and ominous experiences through which English-speaking peoples had ever passed.

In about 1700, some unknown inventor discovered a process for manufacturing cheap gin. Before that discovery, only the well-to-do could afford the luxury of hard liquor. The poor, and the poorly-paid classes of working men and women, drank ale and beer, neither of which was very intoxicating – at least, as they were then brewed. As soon as gin could be bought for twenty-five cents a quart, everybody, including women and children, began drinking it. A Noah's flood of drunkenness swept over the land, and the town's streets became sewers of vulgarity. How vulgar any man can see in William Hogarth's drawings (he was a Grand Lodge Officer), which were not cartoons, but near-photographic reproductions of the daily scenes. In this general inundation of vulgarity, the people discovered a fact that always had been a fact but which they had failed to see. In the end, they discovered that vulgarity is not merely a coarsening of manners but a crime! There came a day when intelligent men everywhere saw with apocalyptic cleanness that the British people would destroy themselves unless this terrible state of general vulgarity were stopped. Accordingly, they lost interest in everything else, including the War in France, dropped everything else, and began a struggle to recover good manners.

Because of one of the most unexpected twists in the history of Freemasonry, our lodges became centers (tho not the only ones) from which that warfare was waged, and because for centuries, etiquette had been an integral part of their work. In his late teens, George Washington prepared a little book on etiquette and learned it by heart because he saw that a man without etiquette could not be fully a man. It was this truth which partly explains his active and abiding interest in the Fraternity. A lodge is a school for gentlemen. The same general social crisis explains why Beau Nash was also an active Mason — enthusiastic in his work for his lodge. Still, more, it explains why Lord Chesterfield, whose name became a synonym for etiquette, was a Worshipful Master, a sponsor of many national leaders when they petitioned for membership, a father of lodges at home and in Europe, and would have been Grand Master had he not been sent abroad as an ambassador.

Vulgarity is a heading toward crime because the principle of it is to harm, spoil, damage, and destroy not only oneself and other men and women but material things and the arts and sciences. In the thick of English-speaking peoples' warfare against this dangerousness in vulgarity, the Mother Grand Lodge wrote and (in 1723) published its *Book of Constitutions*. It was, therefore, not for nothing that alongside its Paragraphs on the Mason and Religion and its Paragraph on the Mason as a Citizen, it placed in the same category of necessity its Paragraph on the Mason and his Behavior.

Chapter XVIII
Masonic Penalties

Symbolic Only

If a man is such that he will take property belonging to others or will assault or murder them if he expects to gain by doing so, it is manifestly unsafe to leave such a man at large. The community must lock him up. It is unpleasant to put a man into a room and keep him there year after year, especially if the room is made of stone and steel to prevent his breaking out of it. He cannot be happy in such confinement, and most men cannot remain healthy. Moreover, it is always a burden on the taxpayers to keep him there because they must feed and house him and pay wages to men to guard him at their own expense. History is full of experiments to avoid hard and costly measures by trying other devices to protect themselves against criminals. It is not an exaggeration to say that nations have been as experimental and ingenious in avoiding having to lock up their criminals as their criminals have been to evade being locked up or to escape after they have been locked up. But the experiments always have failed, and sooner or later, the people have faced the fact that if a man is not safe to be allowed at large, he must not be left to run at large.

The purpose of locking him up, or executing him, is not to make him suffer but to protect the community from him. It is his fault if he is not safe to be left free. It is his fault if it is dreary, painful, or dreadful to be imprisoned or put to death. The men and women of the community do not imprison or execute a man because they are sadists or torturers but because they have no choice. They cannot live without property, and they cannot live if they are always in danger of being murdered or robbed. Therefore, they are compelled to protect themselves, and it does not matter how painful it may be to use imprisonment as a means of protection.

Some men are not criminals but may act unlawfully now and then though they do not resort to murder. The danger in such men is that if they are left alone, they will become criminals, and the community must protect itself against their becoming such. The only protection ever discovered has been to make such men realize they will lose their means of living if they continue to act unlawfully. This is done by fines, meaning that a portion of a man's money or property is taken away from him, or he is excluded (or expelled) from his work. To be thus fined may be exceedingly painful, and it is also painful to inflict fines. In this, again, peoples and nations have experimented with many substitutes. Still, after their experiments have failed one after another, they have always come back to using fines because they have no choice except to do so.

If a man decides to act to create loss or suffering for others (in any of a thousand forms), he does not always do it in the dark or on the spur of the moment. If others discover what he is planning to do, or if they catch him while doing it, they confront him and immediately try to prevent or stop him. Nearly always, the only means they have at hand is to inflict pain on him, and the pain may be physical, emotional, mental, or social — there are times when merely to expose a man (as when he is caught in a lie) is sufficient to stop him.

The Greeks used the word *poine* as the name for "to put an end to" or "to finish." The Latins adopted the word *poena* and gave it the double meaning of pain and "put an end to it." We still use that Latin word in the form of *penalty*. The purpose of pains and penalties always and everywhere is to prevent lawless and criminal acts, and if the prevention fails, we lock a man up because it is too dangerous for him to be at large. And however painful or ugly this use of penalties may be, we must all put up with them because we have no choice except to do so. Lawless and criminal men could end the use of penalties tomorrow by simply ceasing to be criminal or unlawful. Sadly, no known instance of their ever having collectively done so exists.

Communities differ as much among themselves in using penalties as in using anything else in civilization. One community's jail is clean and humane, and another is a filthy chamber of horrors. In one prison, inmates have good food and medical care. In another, they do not. In one community, pain and penalties are measured; in another, they are savage and extreme. But a community's failure to make proper use of penalties is no more an argument for discontinuing their use everywhere than the same community's failure to provide schools would be an argument for doing without education. The one infallible test is: Does a community's use of penalties prevent unlawful acts and keep criminals from going free, or does it not?

During the long period in the Middle Ages when the Masonic Fraternity was taking its permanent form, it was an extraordinary British community that did not have to answer to that test many times over. "Machinery of the law" is a piece of slang or jargon often used, meaning nothing could be less like a piece of machinery. But if the law, or the government, which is the institution of the law, were a piece of machinery, it was never so ill-designed or hard to manage as in Britain early in the Middle Ages. Government is always complex. The peoples of the early Middle Ages were not content to have it complex. Still, they went on to make it complicated by giving a swarm of different "governments" authority to enforce pains and penalties and to do so at the same time:

1. There was "the King's Government," the national government, the civil government, or the common law by which was meant law common to men of every class and everywhere – many different names for the same thing. It could impose penalties on any man, woman, or child.

2. the Church governed using the Ordinances of Religion and by ecclesiastical officers, who could indict, arrest, try, fine, banish, excommunicate, imprison, execute, and often did.

3. many dukes, earls, barons, and other high lords ruled over their region with sovereignty just short of the king's and who had the power of life and death over the men and women who belonged to or served them.

4. There were an uncountable number of guilds, fraternities, societies, sodalities, etc., each of which had its officers, rules, and regulations. Such a guild (to employ that as a generic term) had a monopoly of its work and workers within its jurisdiction. Its officers possessed the

power which had been delegated to them by the civil government to wield authority equal to the scope of that jurisdiction. Such a guild could expel a man, thereby taking away his one means to earn a living, and hence could impose a penalty more severe than any other except imprisonment or execution. It could also suspend a member, fine him, or reprimand him. The Fraternity of Freemasons possessed this guild authority over its members.

5. There were also cities, towns, or boroughs which were self-governing in whole or in part, which had city charters, or had ordinances grounded in sovereignty, and which were almost like small nations and could impose pains and penalties.

To maintain a certain degree of uniformity among these many units of government, the laws of the realm laid down general rules. One was the rule that no man could lawfully act as the officer or deputy for a body of men, however small, or for any borough, community, or realm unless he took an oath. Many of these oaths were made uniformly and often collected into Oath Books. No organization of men could use an oath that violated the general rules governing oaths. Therefore, when the Freemasons exacted an oath before accepting a man into membership or installing an officer, they were doing nothing peculiar. They were doing what the civil law required, and their oaths were of such form or wording as required by civil authorities.

Thurlow Weed, John Quincy Adams, Thaddeus Stevens, Milliard Fillmore, and their colleagues in the crusade to destroy Freemasonry, which the Anti-Masonic Party kept alive from 1826 until the end of the Civil War asserted that American Freemasons had invented a terrible oath that was a sort of blood-pledge that every new member would blindly obey his leaders or officers in whatever nefarious undertaking they would be led into. In the long and leprous history of the persecution by men of their fellow men, it has seldom been that so many men have made so large a mistake about so little. It is still a mystery to his biographers how traveled, and so well-educated a man as John Quincy Adams could have fallen into so infantile a blunder. For one thing, a Candidate does not vow blind obedience to the lodge or his Officers but pledges to observe the Ancient Landmarks and the Rules and Regulations. Had Mr. Adams consulted the first Worshipful Master he encountered, that Master could have told him how little "blind obedience" his members ever gave him! For another thing, a new member is tied into and bound into the fraternity's membership not by an oath but by an obligation, in which an oath is only one ingredient. For yet another thing Mr. Adams could have learned, had he stopped long enough to catch his breath, that "the powerful and peculiar language" which he declared to have frightened the wits out of him was ritualistic and symbolic, that it had originated in the first instance in the Catholic Church and for centuries had been used by priests and theologians, and that the "language" refers not to the penalties used in the Fraternity but to a dramatic and tragical story. Again, what Mr. Adams took to be "the oath" was not peculiar to Freemasonry but, in the Middle Ages, had been used by the churches, monasteries, nunneries, colleges, and guilds all over Britain. It, therefore, had not been invented by American Masons for purposes of secret and conspiratorial attacks on Mr. Adams' Federalist Political Party but had been preserved in the Fraternity by centuries of usage and had been used by lodges generations before either America or Mr. Adams had been discovered. And also, the oath had not been invented by Freemasons for their own peculiar and private purposes but had been framed and used in obedience to laws enforced by the civil government. And finally, "the powerful and peculiar language," even after allowing for its ritualistic and symbolic form, is not and never was a glorification of either crime or savage punishments of crime or an invitation to either. It has always been the complete opposite. It is a picture of the horrors of crime, a denunciation of unlawful or criminal actions. The nefarious things the upside-down Mr. Adams accused the Freemasons of doing were the very things against which the oath was directed. "The powerful and peculiar language" is the measure of its opposition to those things. A Candidate takes an oath not to violate the law but to keep the law.

When Pope Leo XIII attacked Freemasons in his Bull entitled "Humanum Genus" in 1884, he fell into the same blunders of fact as Dr. Adams, except that he fell into them more deeply. He not only accused Freemasonry of being a sort of murder society but also accused the Freemasons of being a "sect." To him, this meant that Freemasons had banded themselves together expressly to destroy the Roman Catholic Church. He felt their "oath" was a pledge to stop at nothing or shrink at nothing to accomplish that purpose. Pope Leo could have learned, had he considered it good form for a Pope to learn from other men, that Freemasons had been using their oath long before the Protestant Reformation. He could have seen that all Freemasons had been Catholic for four or so centuries. He could have discovered that one of the reasons the Freemasons began to use the oath in the first place was in obedience to the Ordinances of Religion, which were laws drawn and enforced by the Pope's church. There was no reason why the Freemasons in the Middle Ages should not use an oath because every other body of men, lay or clerical, used them (priests and nuns take oaths). There was every reason why the Freemasons should use them because the laws of King and Church compelled them to do so. There has never been any reason why the Freemasons should not preserve so old a custom, especially since today, and in the Pope's church, the use of obligations and oaths is too commonplace to attract attention. The Masonic oath is not open to question, peculiar, or unusual, and never has been.

When something must be said by a body of men, generation after generation, and other bodies of men in association with them also must say the same thing, it will become in time formalized, it may even become stylized, and finally, after long usage, it will be given an "orthodox" form. This applies to the oaths and penalties invoked during the Middle Ages and included Freemasonry. By the time these oaths had reached their "orthodox" form, crimes had become classified under two heads, as either heresy in one of its forms or treason in some of its forms. A set of penalties also became orthodox; a man guilty of heresy was burned at the stake, and a man guilty of treason was hanged. Both forms of execution had a few practices in common, such as to "draw" the victim to the place of execution and to mutilate his body before, during, or after his execution. If he was guilty of a capital crime classified as heresy, his tongue might be torn out to warn the onlookers to keep watch over what they might themselves say. If he was guilty of a crime classified as treason, his body might be cut into pieces ("quartered") to exhibit the fact that he had cut himself off from the body of his fellow citizens or that he had had a divided allegiance. A pirate was hanged, or else he was staked down in the sand and drowned by the tide. If these practices were brought into a single picture, it was to indicate the general idea of oaths and penalties. Such a picture was common before 1700 and is often encountered in old books, prints, decorations, emblems, and symbols.

The penalties used by Operative Freemasons were simple in form and few in number: reprimand, fines, suspension, and expulsion. Penalties other than these, less or more than these, would violate civil and religious law.

For while the Masonic Fraternity (like the guilds) had its own officers, rules, regulations, and courts, its officers possessed no authority to try members or penalize members, except such was delegated to them by civil authorities. Had the Fraternity's own officers exceeded the authority thus delegated to them, they would have themselves become subject to trials and penalties in a civil court. That is true of Masonic Officers now, which is a fact that Anti-Masons are careful to ignore. A lodge is permitted by American civil law to reprimand, suspend, or expel a member. Still, if it exceeded those mild and reasonable penalties, its members would be brought into civil or criminal court. (lodge fines were discontinued a century ago.) If any man asserts otherwise in print or public speech, he knows not whereof he speaks, despite knowing better.

CHAPTER XIX
MASONIC CLOTHING

During its first four to six centuries Freemasonry lived and worked among the customs of the Middle Ages. The goal of these customs was directed toward dividing society, religion, work, and public life into separate entities, each one as independent as possible. The larger crafts, trades, arts, and professions were organized under the guild system. That meant that men belonging to any of them had a local guild in their town or city. A local guild had a monopoly on its work or trade and bristled with resentment if any neighbor guild intruded upon its jurisdiction. The general crafts and callings were divided into as many branches as possible. The craft of leatherworkers was divided into tanners, saddle-workers, makers of men's shoes, makers of women's shoes, etc., and each of these local branches had its own local guild. This guild custom had the opposite effect on Britain as a whole.

On the one hand, it united the men of any one craft, and it united these crafts into a national guild system, thereby giving the nation a single organization of both work and workers. On the other hand, it automatically reduced each guild into a local entity with a wall around it.

The word "guild" is here used in a generic sense. There were many forms of organization, called by many names: fraternities, sodalities, clubs, sororities, societies, orders, associations, covens, companies, corporations, etc. Monks and nuns had their orders; lawyers and doctors their societies; women had their sororities in schools; religious cults had covens; literary men had their clubs. If a craft called for special skill or expert knowledge, it might be called a mystery – that name is often given to Freemasonry.

A family itself, if it had a homestead and owned sufficient property, was often an organized unit and could even be incorporated. The old law of entail was enacted for that purpose, and the oldest son, to whom the property was left, was not so much its owner as its trustee. A family itself belonged to one of the "classes" (they were, in reality, castes), and these classes were recognized by the government and had their privileges protected by law. Classes and families were entities, each with its own recognizable identity.

To maintain this general system of many separate social entities, it was necessary to ensure each entity remained unchanged. Otherwise, the religious and civil laws by which they were generally governed would be unworkable. Weavers used the same methods to scour, spin, weave, and dye from one village to another and from one generation to another. Lawyers used the same procedures, forms, regalia, words, and gestures from century to century; so was it everywhere. "New" did not mean something novel, something unheard of, but a new way to preserve something old. Nor did men move from craft to craft or from calling to calling as they do now. They remained in the trade where they had served their apprenticeship, lived in its quarter of the town, and adhered to its customs.

In a modern factory, machines are replaceable, and almost any machine can be used for many purposes. In a Medieval factory, the men were replaceable. During his apprenticeship, a youth learned to use every tool in his guild and to do any kind of work called for by the guild. Therefore, as a rule, the men in any given guild used the same tools, followed the same methods, and worked on the same materials. As some now-forgotten historian once wrote, "the same callouses, the same stoop, the same gait, the same expression in the eyes." The whole outward form of a man was his identification. A stranger could see from a distance to which craft a man belonged and, therefore, could know the quarter of the town where he lived.

It is easy to see from this why it was that in the Middle Ages, clothing, garb, costume, or livery had significance so great. Men in the same craft worked alike. They, therefore, dressed alike, and their work's needs and nature dictated the nature, style, and materials of their clothing. The garb identified a man, showed at a glance, like a uniform, the guild, class, or family to which he belonged. It was a badge that was as true of the Freemasons as any other Craft. Monks and nuns had their habits, lawyers and physicians had their robes, merchants had their apparel, women dressed in the habiliments of their class or station, farmers wore smocks, and men in the crafts wore such clothing as their work required.

Unlike any other family, a family in the upper classes had its family garb and was easy to recognize. Each family had its own color, design, mark, badge, and banner for its men-at-arms to carry. Its servants had their own livery. Anyone in the country, when walking or riding abroad, could identify any man or woman at a distance and see the family to which they belonged. Family designs and colors were woven into the garments in Scotland, hence the old saying, "Every Scotchman wears a uniform." Out of these devices, designs, marks, and badges were developed coats-of-arms, and from them were developed the old art of heraldry. Clothing identified the man.

As said above, this was also true of the Freemasons. They had their distinctive badges and habiliments. We, today, have no official or detailed description of that clothing. We know that it changed a little in detail from century to century. Still, from miniature pictures on manuscripts, stained glass windows, and many random sources, we have accumulated a sufficient number of facts to give us an idea of what it must have been as a general rule. The Operative Masons wore a leather apron, gloves, and a closefitting cloth cap. They may also have worn a close-fitting garment without pockets or flaps to get in the way and soft leather shoes. This costume identified him wherever he went; the square and compasses were his coat of arms. Our Masonic clothing differs much from his, both in materials and designs, but in purpose and principle, it perpetuates his clothing.

Masonic clothing is one of the great themes in the ritual, and as it stands in the ritual, it is of importance equal to that of the history, philosophy, or jurisprudence of the Craft. The theme is most nearly embodied (or expressed) in that magnificent Rite of Preparation, which has many august meanings. That rite as a whole (not confined to Entrance) has within itself a number of particular rites, among them being the Rite of Preparation, the Rite of Discalceation, the Rite of Destitution, the Rite of Entrance, and the Rite of Investiture (including the Apron). The theme of Masonic clothing, which is thus begun in the general Rite of Preparation, is carried on in many forms, including such particular subjects as the apron, gloves, collar, regalia, insignia, badges, modes of recognition, signs, and passwords. The burden of this theme, wherever it appears, in whatever form, always comes down to the fact that any man who comes into membership is to be a Mason and is not to be anything else. He is to do the same Masonic work as others and rise to a level with them, and as far as his lodge is concerned, he is not to be known as anything but a Mason. His clothing identifies him as such.

When the Apron, which stands for the whole of Masonic Clothing, is presented to the Candidate, he is told that it is more ancient and honorable than the Star and Garter, the Golden Fleece, or the Roman Eagle. He is told that it is the Badge of a Mason. He is admonished to wear it with a due sense of the honor it confers upon him, and that if ever he becomes ashamed of it, he will be unqualified to remain in Masonic membership. It may be that these particular phrases were first included in the ritual in the 18th Century, but that fact is unimportant. If they had not been included until last week, they would still be as true as the oldest phrases in the ritual. Such a statement is true because it is one of the oldest truths in Freemasonry. It is a truth that would have been in Freemasonry even if it had never been stated. If the words are taken in their full meaning and in their complete historical sense, there is even a sense that the phrases are almost the whole truth about Freemasonry. They come as close to stating what Freemasonry is as any one sentence could do.

We should remind ourselves of what was said early in this chapter about the castes or classes of Medieval Britain. Those men, those families, and those classes who believed themselves to be "upper," who claimed to rule and to own the country and the men and women in it, looked down on work. They held workers in contempt. It did not matter to them who the workers were or what work they did, or whether it was brain work or brawn work. It was work itself for which they felt contempt. This contempt of workers included the Freemasons who built the cathedrals, the churches, the castles, and the halls, as much as it included ditch-diggers or sailors. Throughout those centuries, the Freemasons refused to admit that this was true. The Freemasons' leather apron was their badge. It was the same sign and proof of rough work. But for all that, the Freemasons were proud of it! They were proud of it because their whole philosophy of life was the opposite of the orthodox philosophy of the whole Middle Ages. The men who held that philosophy looked down upon a man who worked. The Freemasons looked down upon a man who did not work, and they hold to that belief now as firmly and as implacably as ever. It is the marrow in the bones of their Fraternity. The apron is a workman's apron? Yes. Are the gloves workman's gloves? Yes. The collar is the sign of the authority of a Master of Workmen? Yes. Therefore, Masonic Clothing is more ancient than the Golden Fleece or Roman Eagle and honorable than the Star and Garter. If Mason does not hold to this belief, he is not fit to be a Mason if he wears his apron or takes up his working tools with either a secret or a confessed sense of shame as if it were a badge of inferiority. The Craft should have none of him.

When Pope Clement XII issued the first Bull against Free-masonry in 1738, he accused it of being a secret society. When, two centuries later, Leo XIII issued his Encyclicals against it, he repeated the charge and at the same time enlarged upon it. After the Morgan Affair in 1826, the Anti-Masons attempted to destroy Freemasonry in the United States. Their principal attack was upon the Obligation. But soon after, they made the same charge that Freemasonry is a secret society, and they argued that it would not keep itself in secrecy if it did not have something to hide. While these Anti-Masonic diatribes were going on (and for centuries before they began), the actual, known history of the Fraternity contradicted their charges at every point. How could it be said that Freemasons kept themselves hidden in secrecy during these centuries? The Fraternity has compelled every Mason to wear a badge. How could it be said that Freemasons keep themselves hidden in secrecy when men wearing the badges of Masons hold meetings in buildings with signs identifying them as Masonic lodges? It is nonsense.

PART FIVE

CHAPTER XX
VISITING BY MASONS

A modern man or woman goes calling or visits friends casually and easily, often in an informal fashion. To them, "visitor" is a near meaningless word to which thought is seldom given. It was otherwise in the Ancient World. That word was charged with feeling and emotion in the days at the beginning of history. In any of its forms, it always denoted one of the most exciting experiences a man could have because it could be explosively pleasant or excruciatingly painful. The laws covering visitors and strangers stood high among the great laws, and the gods and oracles had much to say about the subject.

Among the Ancient Greeks, a visitor was called *xenios,* a word subtle and many-faceted. Therefore, it was difficult to define. If it changed form, it was because visiting itself was an uncertain and many-sided occasion. The *xenios,* the stranger at the door, was met cautiously, was inspected, and if acceptable, was received with many ceremonies. He was turned away and threatened if not accepted, and the neighbors were warned. If he was received as a guest, it was with a complex rite of hospitality, which was as binding as laws — some of them were laws! At his departure, he received gifts called *xenia.* The fear or hatred of strangers and foreigners was called *xenophobia.*

Among the Romans and other Latin-speaking peoples, a visitor was more often than not *hospes,* or a guest coming into a household was a red-letter day to be celebrated by a festival. The guest would be crowned or have a garland hung about his neck — like the *leis* with which Hawaiians greet their visitors. We have the grand old Latin word in our language in the forms of hospital, hotel, hospitable, hospitality — the last named a fine art of which every housewife is expected to be the mistress.

Among the Ancient Hebrews and other nomadic peoples of the Near East, "visit" had the same meaning as among Greeks and Romans. It also was used with a second and different meaning, almost the opposite of the first. Under the rule of blood revenge, or blood atonement, if a man was murdered, his next of kin sought out the murderer or the murderer's next of kin and "took a life for a life." His finding of the guilty man was a "visit," This dread mission was called a "visitation." Jehovah is described as an evening visitor to Eden in the *Book of Genesis*. The Prophets threatened their recalcitrant people with his dreaded visitations. An echo of that old note of dread lingers here and there in our usage, as when we say that death visits a house, or a community is visited by a catastrophe.

Our word "visit" is of a quieter and humdrum lineage. It continues to carry much the same meaning as *xenios* or *hospes* except that we have given it a twist of meaning characteristically our own. It is a form of the Latin *viso*, which had in it not so much the idea of "to see," as visible, vision, and vision suggest, as it did the idea expressed in our "behold." To behold a thing is more than to look at it; it is even more than to see it (which means far more than to look); it means to keep the eyes held on it or something which holds the eyes on itself — like the serpents in the hair of Medusa. It is a continuous seeing. The visitor does not come to the door to look and then departs, but one who remains to see, and it is you that he has come to see. In the high poetry of the King James translation of the Bible, the translators have it that Jehovah came as a visitor to see, or to behold, the world he had made. In their choice of words, they had the old *viso* in mind, for Jehovah's eyes were held by what He saw, and for that reason, He described it as very good. Continuing in the same veins of language, they describe Him as arriving in the world as a Visitor for a time (He "tented" or "tabernacled"), then returning whence He came—and then coming again as a Resident. In any event and form, a visit means that a visitor is more than a stranger or one who comes to the door. He is not a casual passer-by or one who casually drops in, but one who is invited in and is made welcome. He is one who, for a little while, can advance at least a little way into the circle.

In one aspect, the ritual of Ancient Craft Freemasonry with its Three Degrees is an acted-out philosophy of man in the world of work. The ritual is always saying the same things, but it says it in terms of just one central theme and then of another, one after another. Some of these themes are such as one would expect to find in the Fraternity — relief is one of these — but others are not obvious or to be expected — clothing and wages are examples. Themes of this latter sort must be searched out. A number of the themes are on subjects about which we are all thinking in modern America (cooperation is one), but a number of them are on subjects about which few of us ever think, either much or little. Visiting is one of these major themes in the ritual, which is not obvious but must be searched out. It is not a theme about which we are all thinking and must be thought out by conscious effort. It is in the ritual, as one of its great themes, partly for historical reasons and partly because it belongs to the meaning of Freemasonry.

To repeat what is said in other chapters, men did not visit or travel much in the Middle Ages — the majority of men did neither, except in their neighborhoods. It was because work and activities of many other kinds (including religion) were organized in guilds and fraternities, each confined to its local jurisdiction. A modern workman is free to go and come anywhere in the nation. A Medieval workman was not. He was tied down to his farm, village, or town, and men five miles away, he was a stranger or even a foreigner. To this general rule, the Freemasons were an exception, as they were also an exception in many other ways because any Freemason could come from any other town or even from abroad. Nearly always, they did come from a distance. While they were traveling, they could visit Freemasons or lodges wherever they might come upon them. Not only could they visit, but they were expected to do so. From his traveling brethren, a Freemason could have news about his own Craft. When such a traveler arrived, he was accepted as a guest, as *hospes*, as *xenios*, and treated to hospitality. If he was ill, he was nursed. If in need, he received relief. And there was little danger of spurious visitors because each Freemason had received the Modes of Recognition under the oath of secrecy and could identify himself wherever he went. This freedom to travel and this right to visit were so necessary to Freemasons that they could not have carried on their work without them. Being thus essential, visiting became a Landmark and has continued to be one ever since.

The place of this Landmark in the meaning of Freemasonry is second to no other in either importance or size. A Candidate is made a Mason and in the act of making him one, he is made a Masonic visitor of other lodges. For in the moment of becoming a Mason, he becomes the friend of thousands of men in his community or state and of millions of men in the world. He has never met them, is not acquainted with them, and does not know their names, but he has millions of acquaintances he has never seen. Whenever he meets a Mason and introduces himself as a Mason, he will find himself in a land of amicable fellowship, which was already there before he came — for it to be there is one of the things that is meant by being a Mason.

It is as if each Master Mason had a standing invitation from each lodge in the world to be its guest. He does not need to seek their hospitality; their hospitality is seeking him. This is an amazing fact, especially if a man is an

American Mason. It means that the doors of many, many lodges will be opened to welcome him into their fellowship. If a Mason rightly understands the art and is a member in the sense of being one in his spirit and his interests, as well as in the sense of having his name on the books, he will travel throughout the Craft as often as he can and visit as many lodges as he can.

The rules by which visiting is governed vary in some details from one Grand jurisdiction to another, but not much, and differ nowhere in fundamentals:

1. Visiting is by permission. It is a Landmark that each member in any regular lodge has the right to seek to visit any other lodge in any Communication. Still, he cannot enter the lodge without the Master's consent.

2. If a Mason has already visited a lodge and can be vouched for by the Tiler, he can enter without ceremony but should first write his name in the Visitors' Book.

3. If he is a stranger to a lodge, he can be vouched for by a brother whose avouchment is acceptable to the Master. In most Grand Jurisdictions, an avouchment is acceptable if the voucher has "sat in the lodge" with the visitor.

4. If a visitor cannot be vouched for, the Tiler sends word "through the door," upon which the Master appoints a Committee (or calls a Standing Committee) to examine him. Even after it has reported, the Master is still free to decide for himself, but usually, he will follow the Committee's recommendation. The purpose of the Committee is solely confined to ascertaining if a visitor is or is not a Master Mason in good standing in a regular lodge, not to test his proficiency in the ritual.

5. Refusal. A Master's refusal to grant admittance (and even if a Committee has recommended admittance) should not be taken as a reflection on the visitor. A refusal where the visitor is not at fault ought to be accompanied by explanations and apologies. Still, if there are good reasons

for it, a Master ought to refuse without hesitation. There are many non-personal grounds for refusal, as is illustrated by such cases as when: a lodge is discussing a question private to its members; if a question of discipline has arisen; questions involving relief under circumstances where it is desired to keep the details secret; etc., etc.

6. A voice in lodge. A visitor cannot vote in a lodge or participate in its discussions (unless the Jurisdiction allows it), but he is entitled to the privileges of the floor on request. He should, under proper circumstances, ask for the privilege.

7. Hospitality. A Master acts as host to lodge visitors. He may ask a visitor to salute at the West or the Altar, remain seated when a visitor is received, or advance to the Altar to greet him. He may order the visitor escorted to a certain place, leave him free to find his seat, and ask him to address the lodge. The conditions govern his conduct in each instance at the time. Whatever these circumstances may be, it is proper etiquette for the visitor to accept his reception in whatever form it may take without questioning it, and he should place himself unreservedly in the Master's hands without reluctance or embarrassment.

CHAPTER XXI
BOOKS – RECORDS – HISTORY

Each American Grand Lodge publishes its Constitution, statutes, and general laws in a printed volume called *The Code*. It also publishes its own version of *The Standard Monitor* and may include this in *The Code* or may publish each separately. The *Monitor* is that part of the ritual which is called *The Exoteric Work*; along with it are included ceremonies for Opening and Closing the lodge, ceremonies for Installation of Officers, forms for funeral services, forms for laying of cornerstones, and dedication and consecration of lodges and lodge buildings, forms for documents and reports, etc. A number of Grand Lodges have published Digests of their laws in which compendiums of laws, decisions, and edicts are logically arranged and indexed for ready reference. Many of them have published official histories, biographies, and anniversary volumes. Every Grand Lodge, and as a part of its regular order of business, publishes each year a report of its regular and special Grand Communications in a volume called Annual Proceedings or by some other title that carries the meaning of an annual report.

Thus, if in twenty-five years, a Grand Lodge publishes five volumes such as *The Code* or publishes new editions of such volumes and at the same time publishes thirty volumes, if that is multiplied by the number of Grand Lodges in the United States, it means that Grand Lodges alone are responsible for the publication of thousands of printed volumes in each period of twenty-five years. Since the Grand Bodies of the Capitular, Cryptic, Templar, and Scottish Rites publish volumes of a similar kind, the Masonic Fraternity as a whole in the United States publishes between five and ten thousand printed books every twenty-five years, or from twelve to sixteen thousand each century. Each of these books is authoritative because it is written and published officially. Any question which asks what American Masonry does or does not do, advocates or opposes, believes in or does not believe, can be answered in these volumes and answered nowhere else. In these Grand Bodies, the rank and file of American Masons discuss their state or national affairs, make decisions concerning the whole of the Fraternity, and place themselves on record. Therefore, their decisions and their acts are found exclusively in the reports published by those Grand Bodies.

Each of the lodges keeps a Minute Book, which is what Annual Proceedings are to a Grand Lodge, although it never publishes them. A lodge also has a copy of its By-Laws, usually printed. Also, a lodge may publish a history of itself, a biographical brochure of one of its members, or anniversary volumes. Many lodges print monthly bulletins; a few publish weekly or monthly periodicals or do so in association with other Bodies. Research lodges often publish their treatises and papers in regular or occasional volumes. Several Side Orders, Clubs, Associations, Study Circles, or Research Societies publish booklets and periodicals.

A Grand Body, a local Body, or an auxiliary Body may share in, sponsor, or officially approve periodicals or books written by individual Masons or by voluntary Masonic groups. Books of this category fall below official publications and are not wholly without official sanction. A few books which are written by Masons privately and are published by the author or some publishing house unofficially, are used so often by Masons and by Masonic Bodies and by common consent are accepted as having so much authority that they are to some extent and in effect, official books. Mackey's volume on jurisprudence is the most famous instance. Some Standard Monitors officially used by Grand Bodies were edited and published unofficially by private Masons. If the books published by Grand Bodies, Auxiliary Bodies, semi-official bodies, and private Masons with official or semi-official sanction are added to the books published by Grand Bodies, the total number will not fall far short of 1,000 titles per year.

If a Fraternity is publishing in one form or another, or for one purpose or another, an average of almost three books per day, and if this is the average for one country only (the USA), then Freemasonry prints and publishes not less but many times more than all other societies and fraternities. Professional bibliographers have estimated that more books have been published on Masonry during the past two centuries than on any other subject!

A copy of the Annual Proceedings of a Grand Lodge is a remarkable book. Generations of experience have perfected their form, arrangements, and contents. It contains a list of Grand Officers and Grand Lodge Committees; the Grand Master's Address; reports by Grand Officers; reports of Standing and Special Committees; a report by the Committee on Foreign (or, as it is also called, Fraternal) Correspondence. This last is a Standing Committee of great importance, which as a rule, it has a brother familiar with contemporary Masonic history as either its Chairman or its Secretary. It makes a written report so long that often it occupies a third of the volume. It is a review of the Annual Proceedings of each Grand Lodges with which the Committee's own Grand Lodge is in fraternal correspondence. It is full of friendly but free discussion and criticism and packed with data, facts of unusual interest, statistics, etc. If these Fraternal Correspondence Reports made by the Grand Lodges were collected into a single set of books covering the past half century, they would give us for that period a detailed, day-by-day history of Ancient Craft Masonry in the United States written by itself. As for the Annual Proceedings themselves, containing Grand Masters' Addresses, orations on special occasions, and Grand Lodge Committee Reports as well as the Fraternal Correspondence reviews, they, if incorporated in a single set of books, would contain a great wealth of writings, articles and essays, and speeches and orations on almost every possible Masonic subject.

Alongside these official and semi-official publications is a zone occupied by a species of books that are not official in any sense, or to any degree, which were written by individual Masons and published by the authors or by private publishing houses, but which have so much weight, and are so widely used, and highly regarded that they have so permanently established themselves in

Masonic thought and knowledge that they are almost a part of the Fraternity. These may be described as classic works. Among these are the volumes by Albert G. Mackey, especially his *Encyclopedia of Freemasonry* and his *Jurisprudence of Freemasonry,* the former the most widely used Masonic book in the world, the latter the non-official book most often used by Grand Lodges. The histories written by Mackey, Gould, Hughan, Crawley, Lyon, Singleton, Robertson, etc., are to Masonic history what Thucydides, Livy, Burnet, Gibbon, Macaulay, Redpath, Adams, etc., are to general history. Among these standard works are a few which hold a unique position and may be described as Masonic classics. Any one of them may be out-of-date or may propound some interpretation that the Fraternity has passed over, but in them is a salt, a touch of the ancient literary magics, which keep them alive long after they otherwise would be dead. Just a few are Calcot's *Disquisitions,* Hutchinson's *Spirit of Masonry,* Pike's *Morals and Dogma,* Preston's *Illustrations,* Greenleaf's *Lectures,* etc., etc. These standard books, classics, and near-classics are characterized by their soundness and sanity; that which speaks in them does not grow old. Other Masonic books may — as a few have — become absurd in time, eccentric, or become deviates, or wander too far from the subject. The classic books never do; they are always as healthy as the sea and fresh as the day. If anything true can be said of Freemasonry itself, it is that it tries to be completely open, and so must its books be.

Outside of these three zones of official books, semi-official books, and classic books "stretches a land which bends onward into the illimitable," in which are tens of thousands of books written by Masons for Masons, published year after year over two centuries, in some forty or fifty languages, by men of every persuasion and degree of competency and walk of life. Each has written on his responsibility and often at his own expense, "as the spirit moved him," on every possible question, theme, subject, problem, and detail. A student who has grown gray in this multitudinous literature (perhaps 200,000 titles) knows his way about and can go where he wills without a conductor. A Newly-Made Mason cannot so easily find his path through that wilderness of writing. His best plan is to begin with four or five of the standard books (such as those of Gould and Mackey), upon which millions of Masons have passed their favorable judgments, until he is well-grounded in fundamentals.

With exceptions too few to count, the whole of that literature can be characterized in one short sentence — it has been a labor of love. Our Fraternity has no colleges, universities, faculties, professorships, or foundations for research or publication. It has little or no critical periodical literature. Grand Lodges do not guide Masonic writers, assume responsibility for their books, recognize and rarely reward them. Writers receive no salary, and only a few receive enough pay to cover the necessary writing expenses and hence make a free gift of their time — and also of their gifts. Once a Masonic book is published, it is not reviewed or advertised in non-Masonic newspapers or magazines, is mostly not stocked in bookstores, and must make its own way. If his brethren appreciate his book, there is almost no way for a writer to know it.

The subject about which Masonic authors write their books is more than usually difficult — more difficult than the larger number of subjects taught in the universities. Half of it lies in the Middle Ages, "that little-known land." The field it covers is unimaginably large — far larger than can be believed by a man who cannot read foreign languages. In it are rites, bodies, and subjects like wheels within wheels. It is intimately connected with a number of large subjects outside itself: general history, Medieval history, history of the 18th Century, law, the history of politics, Anti-Masonry in church and state, the guilds, etc.,

etc. Symbolism, a major theme, is one of the trickiest and most treacherous of specialties – and has a way of making the unskilled look ridiculous. As for special and detailed subjects in Masonic history and biography, they are as numberless as the leaves in Vallomribrosa. As for Masonic jurisprudence, it is so stubborn and unlike general jurisprudence that even a Roscoe Pound must learn a new kind of law to write about it.

To write so many books under circumstances so adverse and for results so unrewarding, for so many thousands of men to give so many thousands of years out of their collective lives to do it, and solely "for the love Masons have for Masonry," is, any impartial judge will admit, such a tribute as no other Fraternity has ever received, for these men have not been led to write by the hope of rewards which has pulled them from in front, or by any fear or need which has pushed them from behind. It is Freemasonry itself that has drawn them into it. If here and there such a writer is incompetent, if a book now and then is worthless, if once in a while a literary lunatic is at large, it is unimportant in a literature so many-sided and extensive.

CHAPTER XXII
MONITOR

In the age-long history of Freemasonry, William Preston has the unique distinction of being, likely, the most recognized Mason who has ever edited its ritual. From 2,600 years ago, when Pythagoras wrote a book that his followers copied on gold plates, until now, authors have received their due measure of fame. From the day Longinus wrote his treatise *On the Sublime* until now, literary critics have received their garlands. Even the encyclopedists, that strange tribe who make other men uneasy by their omniscience, have had more than one chapter in history named after them, but in neither the literary nor the memorial arts in general, or special history, has any fame been given to the great editors. Why should they not receive it? They are one of the six pillars which hold up the Republic of Letters.

William Preston was a great editor. Born in Edinburgh, Scotland, in 1742 (when George Washington was ten years of age), Preston learned Latin and Greek before he started school. After dumbfounding his teachers by his precocity, he went to work as private secretary to Thomas Ruddiman – whose name was a synonym for education because he knew almost every language of Europe, living and dead, and a scattering of Oriental languages. After Ruddiman's death, Preston decided to become what was then called a printer but is now called a publisher. After studying the mysteries of that craft for a year, meticulously, as he had once studied grammar, punctuation, and rhetoric, he went down to London. He began work as an editor for James Strahan. Strahan was the head of the best publishing house in the world at the time. Preston became friends with Samuel Johnson, Edward Gibbon, James Boswell, David Hume, the historian Robertson, and the poet Blair, the foremost men of letters in their generation by his social graces as much as his scholarship.

Preston became a Mason in 1762 in London, and it was as if it was what he had been waiting for since he was a boy because he found in himself a native and great affinity for it. Possibly no other man, unless it was England's Duke of Sussex or our own Albert G. Mackey, was ever so completely a Mason (to point to any one of those three would be a sufficient answer to the question, "What is Freemasonry.") He was a member, Worshipful Master, and Antiquity No. 2's leading spirit. From this lodge, which had been one of the original "four old lodges," he ranged far and wide. He visited lodges of every type, talked by the hour, and into the night with "old Masons" who could remember from the days before the erection of the first Grand Lodge in 1717. He assisted in conferring degrees, organized the junta, or the study club, studied old documents, and read anything that might throw light on Freemasonry, particularly its ritual. And whenever he delivered a speech, he held a question box or discussion afterward.

Almost without knowing it, one step at a time, and without having had any conscious purpose to do it, he became editor of the ritual. He found a way to restore portions of the ritual, ignored by carelessness, which was essential to its symmetry and meaning; corrected blunders; restored uniformity from lodge to lodge; found correct words to take the place of incorrect ones; made the degrees as a whole a balanced, consistent, symmetric unity. In 1772, he delivered an epoch-making address while the Grand Officers were present, and in the same year, with the Grand Lodge's official approval, published his *Illustrations of Masonry*.

The Exoteric Work which each Grand Lodge prints in its edition of *The Standard Monitor* may have been, in its original form, written by Preston himself, or he may have collected lectures from here and there, edited them, and arranged them in a system. He may have done either or both with the help or collaboration of his colleagues, but the records are lost. But we know that Thomas Smith Webb took what he described as "Preston's Work," revised it for American purposes at two or three points and incorporated it in his *Illustrations of Masonry* published in 1797 over the signature of "A Royal Arch Mason." In three or four Grand Jurisdictions, Webb's book was adopted as a Standard Monitor by Grand Jurisdictions in the United States. Since, as Webb himself averred, he had used the same Esoteric Ritual that Preston had used, and Preston's Monitor, American Ritual, has ever since been called *The Webb-Preston Work.*

The Operative Freemasons were architects. From the beginning of the Middle Ages to Modern Times, there were architects in Western and Northern European countries and Britain. Still, since our Craft of Speculative Freemasonry originated among British Freemasons, it is to them that we look for our origins. Private or local buildings were made of such material as was locally convenient according to such patterns as best pleased local tastes. But architecture, which consisted of public and monumental structures only, was for some four centuries designed in the Gothic Style. This Style, being living and not one borrowed from museums, had within itself a great potentiality and was infinitely flexible and fertile in detail. Nevertheless, the formula of it, the general principles, and the engineering methods required by it remained fixed. Because they did, many of Freemasonry's practices, usages, customs, and vocabulary remained fixed for the same reasons, generation after generation. The ritual primarily consists of those usages and customs perpetuated or preserved first-hand or second hand by the present Fraternity.

It may be laid down as a rule of history that it is impossible to continue using the same forms of actions and phrases generation after generation without using the monitorial process. When a new man comes in, the old customs must be explained to him. If he is a new man coming into Freemasonry, he can bring no knowledge of it. Therefore, he must be taught. A word familiar in one century is unfamiliar in the next. It may be obsolete; dead words must be spelled, pronounced, and defined. If a man is to take an oath, it is unjust to ask him to take it blindly; the meaning, scope, and penalties must be clearly described. If the new man is to accept a number of tenets or believes in a number of doctrines, they must be expounded. The Monitorial Process is the whole process of defining, explaining, and expounding. There are the original, long-continued usages, customs, and words; there is the accompanying explanation or interpretation, each independent of the other, yet the two are geared together. One is impossible without the other, the relations being like the chapter of the Bible that the preacher reads and the commentary in his own words which he makes on it. Or like the footnotes in an old or a technical book that do not belong to the book's text and must be included to make the text intelligible. The ritual, properly so-called, consists of the usages and customs preserved from early times. The Monitor consists of commentaries, expositions, and explanations designed to assist a Modern man in understanding Medieval words and practices. The work done by Preston and other Monitorialists has always been, therefore, in a literal sense, and not merely in a rhetorical sense, editorial work.

But it has to be remembered that the Monitorial Process is a Landmark in the sense that the ritual would be impossible without it. Preston's own Monitorial Work was not itself a Landmark. The Monitorial Process did not begin with Preston. It began with the first lodge of Operative Freemasons, nor did it end with Preston. When Preston's Grand Lodge approved his Monitor, it fully understood this fact as just stated. It opened the door to other monitorial works in the future because editing, explaining, and expounding will continue as long as Masonry lasts. Webb himself revised Preston. Webb's associates and other Masonic commentators in the United States continued to issue new Monitors. Each new Monitor is a little different from any other one among the editors of such notable names as Mackey, Cross, Barney, Sickles, Macoy, Morris, Simons, etc. After they had used these privately edited Monitors for a half-century or longer, Grand Lodges began to edit and publish Monitors of their own. During the early years of this Grand Lodge editing, the Grand Lodges, like the private editors, departed as little from Preston's original version as they could. But in recent years, it has become increasingly evident that Grand Lodges are yielding to the pressure of our increasing knowledge of Masonic history and are revising their versions of the Standard Monitor more and more drastically.

But whether a Grand Lodge's Standard Monitor is an old version or a new one, it must always have as its principal purpose to make the candidate realize that the Esoteric Work is to have a symbolic meaning. The Lectures and the short monitorial sentences or phrases interspersed through the Three Degrees are threaded on the one theme, "the Operative Freemason did thus and thus and did it for Operative purposes. We also do this and that as they did but do it for Speculative purposes." By the time the candidate has been conducted to the end of the Third Degree, this theme has become familiar to him. To those members who have sat on the sidelines for years, it is so obvious that it may become stale or even boring. But any Candidate – or veteran Mason – can measure the necessity for this theme by picturing the ritual if every Monitorial clement in it were omitted. Would the candidate expect to use his tools on actual stones and wear his apron while doing it? The ritual would give him every reason for expecting to do so were the Monitor lacking, and in such an event, the candidate could find no meaning in such a ritual because he could find no use for it.

This act of clarifying to a Candidate how the ritual is to be understood also makes clear to him why he is being initiated. A factory can train apprentices not for the apprentice's sake but to make them useful to the factory. An army can train a recruit not to give the soldier knowledge or skill for his use but to fit him for its purposes. A lodge could easily have a ritual to serve a similar end so that the Three Degrees would be conferred not for the sake of the candidate but for the lodge's sake – maybe for their entertainment. In this event, a Candidate would suffer himself to be conducted through the degrees without feeling that they mean anything to him. The Monitor is there to ensure no Candidate labors under any such misunderstanding. "This ritual," it says to him, "is yours; this is all being conferred for *your* sake; you are to use it, know and understand, and possess it for yourself." It then goes on to give the principles by which he can understand it.

Again, the ritual could also be a curve that returns upon itself to become a closed curve; when the Three Degrees came to an end, everything in them would be ended. Most fraternities employ such a ritual. Notably a number of college fraternities. Once the initiation is over, the member looks back on it as wholly in the past – he can remember it but is not using it. But the Monitor makes it impossible for any Masonic Candidate to take the ritual of the Three Degrees as a set of temporary ceremonies which will have no place in his future except in his memories. The Monitor continually makes it clear to the candidate that though many of the things he does he is doing for the first time, he is doing none of them for the last time. The Obligation he takes is a continuing Obligation, always in effect. In the First Degree, he is putting on his apron for the first time, but he will continue to put it on whenever he attends lodge. He is taught to salute the East because he can never sit in lodge or have a voice from the floor without saluting the East. There is so much of Masonic life in the ritual. The candidate's initiation might almost be described as the occasion on which a Mason does, says, or becomes for the first time what he will continue to do, say, or be, through countless times in the future. Making a Mason is partly a matter of starting him off. None of the rites, ceremonies, or symbols picture something in the future but are always done. When the candidate dons the apron, he is not rehearsing or practicing. He is actually wearing the apron. If he salutes the East, he is not seeing a picture of what a salutation would be but is then and there saluting the East. The candidate is not made a Mason after the Three Degrees are completed but is being made a Mason one step at a time throughout the degrees.

CHAPTER XXIII
FAMOUS MASONS

To measure and understand the great men of the Middle Ages and even in the Modern Age, an American today must find a way to get outside his mind. What does "great" mean? We often find it difficult to understand how men before the ages of science and mechanical industry could be so much and accomplish so much. They may have been rich, but they were without factories. They may have been conquerors but at the head of troops armed with bows and arrows. We see scholars with neither books nor universities; saints, but surrounded by barbarians; free, and yet in lands filled with slavery! The rank and file of ordinary men always find it difficult to believe that great men are possible because they cannot conceive of a man having so much power and knowledge in himself. How much more difficult was it in the Dark Ages and the Middle Ages when a great or famous man had nothing but himself to use and no resources except his own genius? Roger Bacon had nothing behind him but Oxford, then a third-rate theological academy. He had to learn his science from the Arabs and his geometry from the Freemasons. Yet he gave 14th Century England a new form and a new direction. At about the time Columbus was discovering America, Leonardo was at work in Florence mastering the five arts, two sciences (including aviation), and mathematics, to say nothing of engineering, surveying, navigation, and invention but had little assistance from anything or anyone. Why do we keep the fame of such men alive? It is not to flatter them because they almost all are gone to Valhalla by the time our applause begins — as old Fabre says, "the fiddles arrive too late." Great men are, in fact, creators of civilizations, fathers of peoples, makers of nations, lords of culture, and they are among the most profound of inspirations, for they show to what great heights and to what almost measureless largeness a man can grow.

For some two centuries, Freemasons were the greatest men in Europe. We must understand that fact! We must not permit ourselves out of false modesty or from timidity to ignore it or gloss it over! They were the geniuses who discovered the great Gothic Style, designed and erected the 1,500 cathedrals, built the cities, and altered the aspect of the world; there have never been more towering men! It was because they were so great that their Craft and their Fraternity had projected itself over a thousand years. They did not scheme and intrigue to work as little as possible or to use their minds as seldom as possible but to accomplish as much as possible. No one today can guess what towers of ignorance they battered down to erect their towers of stone or what hells and purgatories of superstition they had to destroy to build beautiful cities. They were civilization-makers, and as Wren said long afterward, they gave the world its face. They did not become jealous if one of their members grew tall above his fellows but gloried in it. "Let Freemasonry be the biggest thing in the world," was their motto, "and let Freemasons be the biggest men in it."

According to A. K. Porter, the first building in which the complete formula of the Gothic Style was used, according to A. K. Porter, was the Abbey Church of St. Denis near Paris, which began in about 1140. Abbot Suger, who had it built, supervised, and probably designed it, was his generation's greatest man in Europe. In his early years, he was an assistant to the Pope, acting King of France during the Crusades, a man of massive learning, the national financier, organizer of armies, and manager of estates stretching to the Channel Coast.

Gothic Architecture did not call Freemasonry into existence, but in the history of the Fraternity, its influence was like that of the moon over the tides. The gravitative touch gave it the direction it was afterward to follow. That style was so new, so different, so unexpected, so undreamed of before, and so marvelous as a work of art that it summoned a new kind of man into the world who was a craftsman, artist, scholar, and fraternalist all in one.

If Suger was the first great Operative Freemason, then Christopher Wren was the last. So that from one to the other, the history of the Craft is like a suspension bridge hung between two great towers. Wren the supreme individual genius produced by England, second only to Shakespeare. The King asked Wren to build anew the ancient St. Paul's cathedral. After London was nearly destroyed in the fire of 1666, he was appointed to administer the rebuilding of the city. In doing so, Wren, not only supervised many lodges of Masons but also perfected that architectural style that is called by his name. This is only a small part of his achievements, like a miniature epic illustration. He was also a superb mathematician. He could draw like an artist and model like a sculptor. He was a doctor and a physiologist and was the first to develop the technique for blood transfusion. He was an inventor; he helped manage international business enterprises; he was an astronomer; he could write better than Samuel Johnson and speak almost as well as Edmund Burke and better than Pitt. As a Latinist, he was so gifted that his orations were used as a textbook at Cambridge.

The few men and women who owned and ruled Britain were also supreme over the arts in the Middle Ages. They permitted no man to own land but themselves, even though he farmed it, so they permitted an artist no credit for his masterpieces. They went by the name of the man who owned them and not the name of the man who had made them. Therefore, a cathedral, minister, or priory was said to have been built by Bishop Wells, Abbe Fulda, or some other high lord, even though the high lord could not read or write and had no more knowledge of architecture than a child. As a result, the great architecture of six hundred years ago was so anonymous that a hundred years ago, writers believed that the Freemasons had made anonymousness a directive among themselves. We now know that this was not true and that the masters had been robbed of the credit of their masterpieces because chroniclers and analysts had been kept servants of the high lords of church and state. They dared give no credit except to those high lords themselves.

As a consequence of the discovery and study of thousands of Borough Records and Fabric Rolls, we have found the names of hundreds of those Masters of Masons who supervised the designing and building of those structures, which are the only actual and visible things still surviving from the Middle Ages. Set in a row, one after another, their navies can mean little to a 20th Century man. But if he could find the time to study their biographies and history, he would learn that each was as salient a personality as Suger or Wren. This would be especially true of such names as William of Sens, Arnold of Croyland, Elias de Durham, Henry Yevele, Walter of Colchester, Inigo Jones, Baldwin of St. Albans, or Palladio. Even Chaucer, the father of English poetry, was the royal administrator of buildings for two years. It is a misfortune beyond measure that our lodge rooms, our Grand Lodge halls, and our memorial buildings have bare walls and empty corridors. They should be crowded with tablets, portraits, and statues of these famous Masons. If they were, the young Mason who enters them would have a different feeling for the antiquity and greatness of the Fraternity.

If to these men of renown of the long Operative Period were added the great names belonging to the Speculative Period of the past two centuries, then the young Mason would find himself surrounded by a great cloud of witnesses. The rooms and the corridors would be filled with living voices, for these latter men also are worthy of any hall of fame. To any Mason who knows the tale of their achievements in the Fraternity and for the Fraternity, the mere calling of their names is like a roll of music: J. T. Desaguliers, founder of the Grand Lodge system, Dr. James Anderson, who gave his name to the first *Book of Constitutions*, William Hutchinson, the first recognized Masonic philosopher, William Preston, writer of the Monitor, Thomas Dunckerley, a builder of the High Grades, Thomas Smith Webb, father of the American System, and the Dukes of Kent and Sussex, statesmen of Masonic unity. The names continue on and on, diversified as the stars on both sides of the ocean: Robert Burns, Sir Walter Scott, Erasmus Darwin, Samuel Wesley, Baron von Hund, Goethe, Martin Clare, Gottfried Leasing, William Hogarth, Dr. Francis Drake, Rudyard Kipling, Sir William Ramsay, Gaedicke, Wolfstieg, Krause, Kloss, Begemann, Lenoir, Voltaire, Lafayette, Chesterfield, Montesquieu, Josiah Barney, Jeremy Cross, Albert G. Mackey, Albert Pike, J. H. Drummond, Benjamin Franklin, Henry Price, Paul Revere, John Marshall, Sir William Johnson, Joseph Warren, W. J. Hughan, G. W. Speth, R. F. Gould, Sir Joseph Warren, Sir Stamford Raffles, A. E. Waite, D. M. Lyon, Chetwode Crawley, E. L. Hawkins, Henry Stillson, George F. Fort, Presidents Washington, Monroe, Jackson, Polk, Buchanan, Johnson, Garfield, McKinley, Theodore Roosevelt, Taft, Harding, Franklin Roosevelt and Harry Truman, Vice-Presidents Colfax, Burr, Tompkins, Breckenridge, Dallas, Fairbanks, Hobart, Johnson, King, Marshall, and Stevenson.

Walt Whitman pled with us in his *Leaves of Grass* to encourage here in America's "richness and variety." If there were a Masonic Hall of Fame (as there ought to be), its thousands of busts, portraits, and tablets would satisfy even Whitman's demands for "richness." It would also astound even Whitman himself for its "variety." Has any fraternity or society ever had in it the room and the catholicity for men so alike in their love of Masonry and yet so unlike among themselves as these, and of hundreds equally individualistic: L. T. Tschoudy, Sam Houston, Mazzini, Kit Carson, The Earl of Moira, Edward VII, George Oliver, H. P. H. Bromwell, Roscoe Pound, Edwin Booth, Rob Morris, The Duke of Connaught, Edwin Markham, Irving Berlin, The Sultan of Johore, Luther Burbank, Edmund Burke, Elisha Kane, Louis Kossuth, James Boswell, Jean Sibelius, Daniel O'Connell, and Parkes Cadman.

Desaguliers was a Masonic statesman, as were Kent, Sussex, Lewis, and Moses Hayes. Albert Pike rebuilt the Scottish Rite and wrote *Morals and Dogma*. Kipling wrote Masonic stories and poems. Lenoir was a scholar in the grand style of erudition. Krause was a philosopher. Drummond was a jurisconsult, an authority on Masonic law, as were also Greenleaf, Lawrence, and Pound. Mackey was an authority on law, an encyclopedist, historian, essayist, and editor. Mozart, Wesley, and Sibelius were Masonic composers. Burns was a poet of Masonry, as also were Markham and Nesbitt. Wolfstieg was a bibliographer. Hughan was a researcher. Parvin was a librarian. Webb and Barney were great ritualists. Lyon became famous as a lodge historian, Speth as a lodge Secretary. Tschoudy was an author of rituals. Waite was learned on the subject of Masonry and occultism. John Jacob Astor was a Grand Treasurer. Washington was a Worshipful Master at the time of his first Inauguration. Andrew Jackson was a Grand Master. Henry Clay was a

Masonic orator, as were O'Connell, Bryan, Marshall, and Cadman. Franklin published the first Masonic book in America. Sir Walter Besant first conceived the idea of lodges for Research. Dunsmore was a Masonic painter. Pope was a great Masonic architect. There is a "richness and variety" among those who stand in our Hall of Fame because there is so much richness and variety in Masonry. It is a world; it also fills the world and, at innumerable points and places, challenges any Mason to accomplish as much as he can.

The early Greeks continually used the word *hubris*, now obsolete and forgotten, except among men who love ancient languages. In a general way – for it is untranslatable – it meant a certain insolent, insulting, arrogant anger. It was such as a king might feel when angered at a lowly subject, a scorching blasting inescapable and destroying anger. The Greeks used it for their gods. If a man did any perfect work, which was a masterpiece, and which both attracted and excited the public, there was a danger that the gods, happening to look down on it from Olympus in the lulls between their brawls and quarrels, might become jealous of it, and search out the maker of it to destroy him out of jealousy. Therefore, artists and skilled craftsmen always left some slight defect in their work as insurance against hubris. Our own Pueblo and Navajo act according to the same doctrine when they never quite complete a rug or bowl pattern. Out of it came the doctrine (not a true one) that perfection is impossible. It is a high-flown ideal, a Holy Grail forever moving just out of reach, and men must go according to the Pragmatist's motto of "ever, not quite."

It is a child-like doctrine, yet it reflects an indubitable fact that any man may encounter in any walk of life. It is notorious that a king cannot bear to have another too close to the throne. But not kings only but lords of business, holders of public office, actors, beautiful ladies, and darlings of the public, and many others. A Newly-Made Mason, as he pushes ahead into the unknown countries of the Craft, need never be afraid lest he falls victim to hubris. It is too much to say that Lodge Offices were expressly designed to guard the lodge against that evil. But it is as if they were; lodge leaders who are not "elected persons," victorious political party candidates, but are Installed Officers. They cannot tailor their offices to fit themselves, use them to reward their friends or belabor their foes. Their prerogatives are defined and fixed by law. Moreover, they hold office usually for one year only. If a Worshipful Master were to hold office as a reward for intrigue and could hold onto it *ad vitam.* He would become a god, jealous of other men more talented than himself. He would chop off the top of a tree for no other reason than that it has grown taller than himself.

No, Mason needs to be afraid to climb high for fear lest somebody pull the ladder from under him. If a Josiah Drummond brings into his lodge such a knowledge of Masonic law as no man there can rival, the Master will not scowl him away from the East. No "Boss" will stifle that golden voice if Henry Clay sits on the sideline. Ecclesiasticus' call, "Let us now celebrate famous men," has been quoted in Masonic lodges, and Masonic books times without number. But lodges have not stopped short of quoting it. They have worked to have it come true. It is said that a metaphor must not be pushed too far or be expected to "go on all fours." So, is it also with a symbol? A Mason is to glance at it with a quick and perceptive eye but is not to ride on it. It will not violate these two reflections if we note that while a lodge has the floor and four walls, its ceiling is nothing but the starry-decked canopy, the sky, and the heavens. A lodge member is in a place of his own or is in a station and cannot go about where he wishes. He is not footloose, but he can grow as tall as he has it in him of either will or ability to grow.

Why does the lodge pitch its ceiling so high? Because it must. It needs a world of room. It is not a little club into which men creep to get away from their wives. It is not a benefit to society. It is a world power with its own place and function among other world powers. The world is its stage; its purposes are as wide as man. Its work is so great that the greatest men can never exhaust it, and its confines would not crowd Confucius, Moses, Zoroaster, Pythagoras, and Aristotle. There would be no long Honor Roll of Famous Masons on one side of the medal were the greatness of Freemasonry itself not inscribed on the other. If any critic is tempted to charge these words to an enthusiasm for the Fraternity, he can ignore what Masons say and turn to read what history says. If he does, he will discover that history says the same thing.

Let no Newly-Made Mason enter upon his Masonic labors with the misgiving that it will, after all, prove a small matter, and he may soon wear it out. He is not in a small and innocuous social club. If it had been either innocuous or a club, Mussolini would never have felt the need to clear it from in front of him before setting up his Fascist tyrannies. Franco would not have condemned each Mason in Spain to ten years in prison before losing the plague of his Phalangist rebellion. Hitler would not have placed its obliteration high on his agenda of Nazi destruction. Petain would not have stopped to sweep it out of France before setting up his Vichyism. It would not have been one of the main issues of World War II.

CHAPTER XXIV
THE INDIVIDUAL LODGE

It is sometimes mentioned in general conversation by non-Masons, that Freemasonry is something of a collection of beliefs, doctrines, or ideas. It is seen as a philosophy or belief system rather than an organization. I find this to be extraordinarily interesting. It is extraordinary because it is wholly mistaken. It is interesting because it shows how little Masonry is understood among many non-Masons. For some four centuries, the word "Freemason" was understood only as an "Operative Mason." The old builders were men, not ideas. And this is the first fact to be stated in any description or explanation of a Masonic lodge. Freemasonry is composed of members who are flesh-and-blood. They meet in actual rooms and buildings. The place where Masons meet is called a *lodge*.

A lodge is a collection of Freemasons, or its membership, as well as where they meet in any given community. Wherever such a lodge exists, Freemasonry exists in that area. To it applies the principle of all or nothing. A lodge must have a charter, a quorum of members, and a full complement of officers. A lodge must confer three degrees, it must have the means to carry out Masonic purposes, and act according to the rules and regulations of its Grand Lodge. If one is a member of a regular lodge anywhere, then he is recognized as a Freemason by other regular lodges everywhere.

Freemasonry is self-contained. It is uniquely itself. Members of a lodge are not permitted to do any work except Masonic work. By this it means that a lodge is for the business of the lodge. A lodge would not devote half of its meeting to its own business and the second half to the business of a local civic club.

If a certain number of Master Masons who are in good standing, and regardless of where their lodges are located, find themselves living near each other, they may decide among themselves to set up a new lodge. They can petition a Grand Lodge for official permission if they find themselves of one mind. If they are in a region over which one Grand Lodge exercises exclusive territorial jurisdiction, they petition it. If two Grand Lodges divide the region in which they live, they can petition the Grand

Lodge of their choice or let the Grand Lodges decide between them which is to receive the petition. If they are in "open territory," and no Grand Lodge exercises any degree of jurisdiction over them (extremely rare), they can petition any regular Grand Lodge anywhere in the world.

If the petitioners prove to the Grand Lodge that their petition is just and wise, the Grand Master of that Grand Lodge will grant them a *Dispensation*. This is the authority to operate, which is limited to a fixed time. In the United States, such a lodge is said to be *Under Dispensation* (U. D.). It is also described as an *Inchoate Lodge*, which means incomplete.

If the lodge Under Dispensation proves to deserve a charter, it will receive one. In this, it is given its official name and an official number; also, its jurisdiction is named. The lodge is then consecrated, which means that everything in it is set apart for Masonic uses and, at the same time, is officially accepted for those uses. Its room or building is dedicated, by which it is publicly declared that the premises are to be used for Masonic purposes. Its Officers are installed, meaning they are officially established in their places and are given oaths that bind them to discharge certain duties. Such a lodge is organized, articulated, and structuralized (there is a choice of terms) from top to bottom. Nothing is left hanging loose; nothing is fluid, and there is no uncertainty as to what to do. It is often said in the outside world that Freemasonry is something mysterious, dark, secret, or occult; the impression left on the mind by these words is that it is mystical and vague. The largest mystery in that statement is the mystery of why anybody ever says it because nothing could be less vague or mystical than a lodge's form of organization. Its dispensation and its charter are written prescriptions. Every detail of it is fixed and defined. Any member in it, even the newest member, can see the whole of it stands before him as definite and as plain and as understandable as a building.

In his *Jurisprudence of Freemasonry* (which has been more often used by American Grand Lodges than any other Masonic book), Dr. Albert G. Mackey lists "the rights and powers of a lodge" under fourteen heads. They are reproduced here in the form of brief, running commentaries:

A lodge has the right to retain the possession of its own charter. If a lodge cannot hold a Communication unless its charter is present, if it cannot confer a degree, accept a member, or be represented in Grand Lodge without the authority inherent in the charter, then the lodge cannot exist without it. But according to the same rule, a lodge cannot be dispossessed of its charter if it is lawfully held. The Grand Lodge cannot recall or suspend it except for cause after due hearing and with due process of law. Neither a clique nor a schism can alienate it, and no other lodge can take it away. The power which compels a lodge to have a charter confers on it the inalienable right to keep it. Furthermore, a charter protects a lodge against un-Masonic or anti-Masonic practices among its members and against alien, unwarranted, or offensive interference from outside. The last is true because the authority of a lodge charter is recognized by civil law.

It is legally authorized to carry out all the work of a regular and duly constituted lodge. It never needs to ask permission to carry out any of the work or duties of such a lodge because it possesses ample authority. For special or emergent work, or for work which may be called in question, it must ask advice, decision, or permission from the Grand Master or the Grand Lodge, but never for its regular duties.

A lodge's relations to its Grand Lodge are (as modern logicians would describe it) multiterminal and, therefore, cannot be stated in a sentence. In the first instance, a Grand

Lodge is constituted by three or more regular lodges. In the second instance, the moment a Grand Lodge comes into existence, it brings with it its sovereign power and the lodges which constituted it are, from that moment, subordinate to it. In the third instance, lodges are constitutive of the Grand Lodge because it is only as they are members of it that a Grand Lodge exists, and as Constituent Lodges, they have the indefeasible right to be represented in it by their Worshipful Masters, and (as their constitutions may read) by one or both of their Wardens.

If a lodge were a separate and independent body, free to go its way, and was in a hurly-burly of competition or a struggle for existence, a foe could stifle it by cutting off its supply of new members. A lodge is protected against the destruction of having its supplies cut off by enemies or circumstances by possessing the perpetual and inalienable right of admitting new members by initiation or affiliation. (The Mother Grand Lodge of 1717 once attempted an innovation of their Landmarks by adopting a rule that Masons could be "made" in Grand Lodge only, but the rule was quickly rescinded.)

A lodge has the right to choose out of its membership its elective Officers. The elective Officer or Officers have the right to choose the appointive Officers. This is one of the cornerstones of the Masonic system because it is plain and unequivocal proof that a lodge has the same absolute sovereignty within itself and over its jurisdiction that a Grand Lodge has over its jurisdiction. The body of members is a legislative body within a restricted area, but it is the Worshipful Master who rules and governs. He is assisted by his Wardens and helped by the Deacons and Stewards. The Secretary, Treasurer, and Tiler have no governmental functions. No lodge is ever ruled and governed by either the Grand Master or the Grand Lodge. If a Grand Master were to usurp the permanent function of Lodge Officers, the aggrieved lodge could cite him for

Masonic trial before Grand Lodge. If a Grand Lodge usurped them, other Grand Lodges would withdraw their recognition from it. A lodge rules and governs itself. It does so through its Officers and by vote of the members.

A lodge has the right to *Install* its Officers. The Ceremony of Installation means that each office's place or station, duties, rights, and prerogatives are in the Landmarks and are fixed and defined by law. They cannot be amended by discussion or altered by vote of the members, nor are they revised or altered by the Officers themselves. An Officer is an incumbent. He has complete authority to discharge the duties of his office but no authority to decide what those duties are, and his oath is to his office. Each Officer occupies his office continually during his term, twenty-four hours a day, seven days a week, throughout the lodge jurisdiction. He is not one who was installed but is in continual installation and therefore is called an Installed Officer.

A lodge makes its own by-laws. These have the same absolute and final authority within their field (or jurisdiction) that the constitutional and general laws of the Grand Lodge have in theirs. A Grand Lodge may prescribe a form to have uniform practices among its lodges, and it may name the heads to be covered by a lodge's by-laws, but no Grand Lodge can write by-laws for any lodge (though uniform by-laws may be suggested and recommended). A lodge can have provisions in its own by-laws peculiar to itself because no two lodges work under the same circumstances, but the provisions must not violate the Landmarks. They must be consistent with Grand Lodge laws.

Dr. Mackey states that a lodge has the right "to levy a tax upon its members." Jurisconsults have since disagreed with Dr. Mackey in his use of the word "tax" because they hold that there is little similarity between dues collected by a lodge and taxes levied by a state. A tax is a charge on its citizens imposed by the government; dues are a lodge member's pro-rated share in the year's expense of running the lodge. When members decide by the ballot what expenses will be incurred, they decide in so doing and, to that extent, what their dues shall be. Taxes are levied against funds and properties of fixed value; dues are levied against no funds or properties. Their basis is not in units of fixed value but in decisions made by the lodge. It is a Landmark that a lodge member must pay his equal share of his own lodge's expenditures, and he can be suspended or expelled if he refuses to do so.

If, when acting within their rights and prerogatives, the body of members votes to have the lodge act in a certain way, and if what is voted entails action by the Master, the Master must take that action. He cannot appeal to his own members. But when he acts to carry out the duties inherent in his office, no appeal can be taken from his act to the lodge floor. If a Master is guilty of malfeasance, neglects his office, or acts to endanger his lodge's existence or good name, the members can appeal his decisions or actions to the Grand Lodge. Subject to the approval of the Grand Lodge, a lodge has the right to select its name (if not a duplicate of an operating lodge's name). A number is given to it by Grand Lodge. It can designate or change the time and place of its meetings as provided in the by-laws. It has complete penal jurisdiction over its members and summary penal jurisdiction over members of other lodges residing or visiting in its jurisdiction.

Any organized body of men which works under general and constitutional laws, by-laws, rules, and regulations, which are fixed or permanent, always finds that new occasions arise, unpredictable events, and unforeseen emergencies, which require action or decision but are not covered by laws and rules; and so is it with a lodge. No more interesting question can be asked of the jurisprudence of any organized body than how it provides for these contingencies. In some organizations, such questions go to some final body or committee, which is, in principle, a supreme court or a court of last appeal. In others, they go to some officer. A large number of methods are in use, and among themselves, they are unlike each other not only in form but in principle.

Freemasonry's method for deciding a question not included in already-existing laws and rules is to put the whole Fraternity at the questioner's disposal and then let him decide it according to his wisdom and intelligence. The means at a lodge's disposal for deciding on unclassifiable or unprecedented questions are almost numberless, as is shown by a typical but partial list of them: A Master can use his own judgment; the officers can confer among themselves; it can be discussed and decided on the floor; the Master may confer with Past Masters or his most experienced members (their role in a lodge is larger than it may appear to be); the Grand Master or other Grand Officers may be consulted; it may be carried into Grand Lodge; the lodge may seek for light in Masonic literature; the question may be answered by pure reasoning; it may be answered temporarily, tentatively, experimentally; etc. No lodge is ever brought to a dead stop because it has run out of laws and rules; in the last resort, it can always entrust itself to its members' intelligence, wisdom, and character.

CHAPTER XXV
THE MASONIC COMMUNITY

If when a man came into Masonry, he found nothing in, or connected to it for his wife, his family, his relatives, and his friends, he could not find much in it for himself. If Freemasonry consisted of nothing but lodge meetings, if the Masonic life were a matter of attending lodge once a month or once every two or three months, Freemasonry itself would not have much to give him. It has always been the way of the Fraternity whenever it has established itself in any village or town or jurisdiction to establish itself not as a certain number of individuals, separate members, or even as a lodge but to establish itself as a Masonic Community. This Masonic Community embraces not only individual Masons but also a Mason's wife, family, and relatives. It is this community which is the fundamental unit of the Fraternity.

When Operative Freemasons arrived at the site of a building that would take them years to construct, they spent the first few months settling in and organizing themselves. Their earliest step was to find homes to live in, and if no houses were available, they took the time to build them. In some instances, these comprised a whole village; in a few English communities, those "Masonic villages" still exist and are in use. If their work was to be in a large town or city, they would have a place together called a "quarter," which might comprise a "ward." On the work site, the craftsmen erected a building to meet in, keep their tools in, and possibly work in for certain tasks. This building was called the lodge. In many places, they erected a second building to draw plans, make templates and models, and keep books. They lived together as a group; they worked together as a body. Their rules and regulations governed them at home and work, and the Master of Masons was their Master twenty-four hours a day. The quarter in which they resided was called the Masonic Community.

When a youth entered as an Apprentice, he entered this Community. He became a member of the Fraternity with the status of apprentice and, as such, was bound by a legally drawn and executed indenture. His first duty was to study and learn. It was necessary for him to master his tools, understand the materials in which he was to work, and obey his master. The rules and regulations required that he report at the same time as the others and put in as many hours of work as possible. But this youth also was to live in his master's household as if he were a foster son. Therefore, he had to be personally acceptable. No family would accept into its circle for seven years a boorish, ill-tempered youth. Therefore (as we learn from the Old Charges), he was taught manners and politeness. He was not to disturb the neighborhood, embarrass his brethren at work, or discredit the good name of the Craft. He was to be made into a Mason. But he could never become a Mason merely by learning to use tools. He had also to become a peaceable member of the Masonic Community.

The Operative Freemasons were highly accomplished in one of the most grueling and demanding of crafts. It has puzzled many modern Freemasons how such workers could have also found a place for fraternalism, fellowship, charity, religion, and thought. The facts about the Masonic Community explain that puzzle. Men who live together, as well as work together, have everything in common. The men who lived next door to each other at night and worked side by side during the day did not dare to quarrel. It was too disastrous. They could not be indifferent to each other even if they wished because, whether at home or work, they were kept continually together. Their fraternalism was not merely a matter of feeling friendly toward each other; it also was a matter of being able to work with each other day after day and year after year.

The intellectual side of Freemasonry was equally a necessity. Knowledge, skill, and intelligence were not luxuries. They could not be left to a few specialists and experts but were called for in each man during each hour and at every point. In the modern building craft, a workman can leave geometry, designing, and planning to men in architects' offices. They can leave carving, sculpture, and painting to artists and can leave engineering to factories and engineers. But in Operative Freemasonry, each and every workman had to be a master of each of these arts. When a present-day Masonic writer states that the Freemasons were the most intelligent, best-educated, and greatest men in Europe for two or three centuries, a non-Mason will write it off as boast. But the Masonic writer is entirely correct in what he says. The great mass and pressure of this intellectual and artistic life was a part of the Masonic Community, belonged to it as much as the lodge.

Men in the building crafts now do not live near each other, except accidentally. If a family member is ill, a physician or a nurse is called in, or the patient is sent to the hospital. If a man dies, his widow and orphans must shift for themselves as best they can. During the evenings and on Sundays, one member of the trade may not see another member. The opposite was true of the Medieval Freemasons. They helped each other in times of illness; they spent their evenings and Sundays among themselves. The families and the men went to church together, celebrated holidays, and walked in procession to the Saints' Chapel. They stood together at the graveside — no widow or orphan was left alone. A Freemason lived and worked for the Masonic Community, as well as in it. What we now call their fraternalism was neither separate nor separable but belonged as much to Operative Freemasonry as the use of tools or stones. There is no mystery why they left so much fraternalism to us Speculative Freemasons because the first lodges of Speculative Masons inherited not only the symbols of the old Operative Lodges but the whole Masonic Community. Wives, families, children, widows, orphans, relatives, and friends were in the circle of the Fraternity from the beginning. If a Freemason grows weary of "Lodge Masonry," he does so for a sound reason because Freemasonry was never intended to be cut down to the limits of the lodge and its work. The Masonic Community does not exist for the sake of the lodge. The lodge exists for the sake of the Masonic Community. The lodge is the point. The Community is the circle which gives the point its position and meaning.

Even if a Mason knew nothing of the history of the Fraternity, he could discover these facts by reason alone if he were to examine the structure of the lodge organization. The lodge is a lodge, but Freemasonry is a society. The wives, widows, orphans, and families of members are present in the Obligations. The Lesser Lights are a picture of the Fraternity as it is locally, by night (the Moon) and by day (the Sun), and the Worshipful Master rules and governs during both. So that he is not only the Worshipful Master of the lodge but of the whole society as it is in its local jurisdiction. He is assisted during working hours by the Senior Warden and during the "night," which is the society after the Communication is closed, by the Junior Warden. The Rules and Regulations (they ought to be read to every lodge at least twice a year) are for the families as well as the men and include the hours when Masons are not in the lodge as well as when they are. The lodge's structure presupposes not merely a lodge building, a meeting once a month, but a continuing community that never closes nor even stops for a recess. It should be a community where Masonic families ought to be knit together, and Masons ought to be fellows outside the lodge Room as much as they are in it. It should be a community in which the members and their families should share in society, and social life, of their own.

One of the most unfortunate of the many consequences of the Anti-Masonic movement, which began in 1826 and did not entirely spend itself until the 1870s, was to throw the leadership of the lodges into the hands of a generation of men who were not Masonic statesmen. They refused to learn or to read. They opposed or obstructed the normal and healthy means of enlightenment within the Craft. Their whole theory of Freemasonry was that it consisted of a lodge only, and they walled it as tightly as they could, and they cropped off or dug up every growth of the Masonic life which could not be tied down to officialism. They insisted that Freemasonry is a secret society. They locked their secrets, and the lodge Room became as bare and unlovely as a monastery cell. But Freemasonry itself took revenge upon a generation of leaders who, in their timidity, denied the reality and the rights of the Masonic Community, for it sent its roots out under the walls, and from them came all manner of growths, good and bad, which under a wise leadership would have had a normal growth inside the Fraternity itself. The Order of the Eastern Star was set up as an Auxiliary for the members' wives and relatives. To this day, no man can explain why it was necessary for Masonic families to go outside of Freemasonry to do it. And from the Eastern Star came many side orders of its own. Also, there came into existence the Shrine, the Grotto, the Order of DeMolay, and along with them, a national proliferation of Masonic clubs of a hundred kinds and names. Not one of these extramural, extra-curricular, or quasi-Masonic associations would ever have been constituted. In no instance would any need have been felt for one of them had we in the United States kept firm hold of the ancient and basic fact that it is the Masonic Community as a whole and not the lodge only, which is the basic unit of the Fraternity in any local jurisdiction. It was the basic unit for the very good reason that the Community, with the lodge at the center of it, would have satisfied the needs and desires which these extramural societies and clubs were brought into existence to satisfy. On the other hand, the lodge itself would not have suffered mutilation; its Communications would have been more like community occasions and less like business meetings – never in its history has it been presupposed that Freemasonry could be reduced to business meetings!

The word "sociology" was coined by Auguste Comte in 1839 as the name for what he hoped could be developed into a science. It has since become familiar in every college curriculum. The word "society" was coined by nobody. It is a Latin word translated into English, but it is far older than Latin, and in one form or another, stands in every language of the world and has done so from the beginning. It is here used in that ancient and universal sense and not in the narrow and almost jargonistic sense that Comte tried to give to it. When a man enters the world, he comes into it by birth, and there is no other way for him to enter it. Birth involves a father and a mother, one as much as the other, and it also usually involves, with equal necessity, brothers, and sisters. The father, mother, brothers, and sisters are a family. This family must be housed, and the house and the family are home. Meanwhile, the father and mother have parents and grandparents of their own, brothers and sisters of their own, uncles and aunts, nieces and nephews. The circle of men and women thus linked together are blood relatives. When the sons and daughters become adults, they marry; when they do, their wives and husbands belong to the family in the same sense as those who were born into it, and they, in turn, have their own blood relatives. They and their blood relatives are relatives by marriage. (The only correct meaning of "relative" is "one tied by blood or marriage.") Out of birth and marriage, there arises a network of relations by blood or marriage: this network is meant by the word "society." Any other kind of association should be called by a different name.

The Masonic Community of the Operative Freemasons had a vitality, a scope, and a meaning so immense that it perpetuated itself century after century. At present, it exists in the form of our Speculative Fraternity. It is now clear why this was true. The Masonic Community was built upon society. It consisted of the Masons, their blood relatives, and their relatives by marriage. Had it consisted of the Masons or lodges only, it would have perished when the guild system was broken up and destroyed after the

Reformation. It is equally clear that lodge and Grand Lodge statesmanship must continue to build on that same foundation. Society will not be denied; if put out of the door, it will come back in through the window, and if it is walled out, it will send its roots under the walls. Who would wish to see it shut out? Who would ask to have the Masonic Community denied or destroyed? If Freemasonry were cut down to the crabbed limits of lodge business once a month, a man might give a night to it four times a year or give a few dollars to it once a year, but he could never give his heart to it because it would have no heart in it.

Chapter XXVI
Freemasonry's Place in the World

The world is the earth and the sky with the atmosphere between the two, plus the people in it and what they have made of the earth by their own work. People are never melted down into a general abstraction called mankind (or "humanity"). Each individual human is "this particular person." Each is indestructibly individual, absolutely unique, and no one is interchangeable with another like the parts used in mass production. This is true because each of them is unmistakably an "I."

Look at Freemasonry. It happens that the very individuality of the members consist, in part, of their being sons, fathers, brothers, uncles, and nephews. Each is in a family; the families are related by blood and marriage, constituting society. These men work in associations, live in communities, and are linked in peoples, nations, institutions, associations, unions, fraternities, and other organizations without numbers to keep themselves thriving. Freemasonry itself is a fraternity. The question is, where does it belong among the other groups and associations? What have they to do with Masonry, and what does Masonry have to do with them? Where is Masonry's place in the world?

When men in the United States, Canada, Britain, and elsewhere set about answering a question of that type, they almost invariably bring to bear upon it a habit of thinking or reasoning which has become so ingrained that few of them are conscious of it. They may be bemused to discover that such a habit of mind would strike some as being a very odd sort of reasoning. You first divide everything into classes; thus, horses of every possible species and variety are put into a class called "horse," buildings of any possible shape, material, or purpose are put into a class called "buildings;" wheat, corn, rye, oats, barley, and similar edible grains are put into a class called "cereals;" and so forth until everything is put into some "class" or other. Next, you make up a description, inventory, or resume of any of these "classes," which is supposed to define it. That done, you can then have your ideas, theories, or feelings about the "class," and this means when carried into practice, you carry about a ready-made judgment, a feeling about a "class" which you can apply to any thing which you believe to belong to it.

How this works out is too familiar to call for many illustrations. There is a class of practices called "religion." A given man has "made up his mind" about religion, believes in it or does not, likes it or does not, and has a set of ideas or theories about it. When he encounters something which he takes to be a particular instance of religion or is told that it is or guesses that it is, he has judged it beforehand because he brings to bear upon it all that he carries about in his mind on religion. A similar example is the "class" of "politics." If a man has "made up his mind" about the class called politics, he has necessarily made up his mind about any given man or activity he believes to belong to that class. If he hates politics, "recognizes politics to have some usefulness," or likes politics, his general judgment will also be his particular judgment. A third and last example is so familiar and inclusive that it could easily have been sufficiently illustrative if only it had been used. It is that of the classification of men. A man divides men into such classes as "upper," "middle," or "lower;" the successful, the unsuccessful; the rich, the poor; conservatives, liberals, etc. If he hates or likes or approves or disapproves, or supports or opposes any of these "classes," he will extend his ready-made judgment and feeling to a man the moment he meets him.

This habit of thinking began in the Middle Ages with Scholasticism. The scholastics built the theory out of what they believed to have been taught by Aristotle, the Greek philosopher whom they worshipped only this side of a god. This Aristotelianism is now wholly discarded by trained thinkers, mathematicians, logicians, philosophers, scientists, and theologians, and it was discarded because it was demonstrated to be false to facts. We can take that there are kinds of things; we can also take that for convenience, plants and animals may be classified according to order, family, species, and variety. But the words kind, order, species, etc., as used here, do not mean what "class" means or anything similar. No man should ever come to a thing or question about things with his mind made up beforehand. He must first obtain the facts and afterward let the facts make up his mind for him. Otherwise, he can be neither truthful nor rational.

This technical and possibly too recondite discussion was necessary for a true answer to the questions of Freemasonry's place in the world. Any reader of the body of Masonic literature and, more significantly, of books written before the first decades of this century knows that many of the writers who set out to explain Freemasonry and to give its place in the world used the Aristotelian habit of thinking to do it with. They took it that all groups or associations fall into classes. Among these are such classes as government, schools, churches, fraternities, clubs, philosophies, occultisms, etc. They then argued that Freemasonry necessarily belongs to one of these classes. They concluded that whatever is true about the class it belongs to is true about Freemasonry. What class does it belong to? An analysis would probably show that our writers have given approximately sixty answers to that question. But since we don't need a catalog of answers but a clear understanding of how the method worked, two examples will be sufficient, one from an old writer and one from a recent writer.

The Rev. George Oliver was a prolific writer and was the Craft's most widely read author for at least one generation. He was wordy and diffusive, was often uncertain of his mind, and was often inconsistent with himself from one book to another. But any reader of the whole body of his books will find that Oliver believed that among the many classes of things is a class that in his generation would have been described as "the handmaidens of religion." Once this is seen, it is easy to follow Oliver's reasoning: "A handmaiden of religion," he argued, "is any society or association which is not a part of the church but exists to assist or to support the church. It is a religion, but not a dogmatic religion. Freemasonry is a handmaiden of religion; therefore, Freemasonry is a religion, but is not a dogmatic religion." The second example is that of a writer who is for his sincerity everywhere deeply respected and for his great learning everywhere profoundly admired. This writer is Arthur Edward Waite, who, during a lifetime devoted to the Fraternity, gave it a long series of books, some of which are Masonic scholarship at its best. What is here said refers only to his theory of Freemasonry's place in the world, which in the present writer's own words, may be briefly stated: "There is a class of religious practices (or experiences) called mysticism; Freemasonry is a religious mysticism; whatever may be the place belonging to religious mysticism in the world is the place belonging to Freemasonry." It is obvious that these two answers – and it would be equally obvious of the other fifty-eight or so – all follow the same patterns of reasoning: it is assumed that there are a certain number of classes of associations, societies, etc., that each of these is to be described, judged, defined, appraised in a certain way; and that whatever is true of the class of association to which our Fraternity belongs is true of it.

But it would be misleading to let this analysis stand to give the impression that only Masonic writers have ever used this pattern of reasoning. It has been used equally often by non-Masonic writers, and their results have often been surprising enough and sometimes have shocked us. The Roman Catholics long ago, and officially, classified our Fraternity as a *sect*. They define a sect as some organization, presumably religious, which exists for the express purpose of destroying, dividing, or troubling the Roman Church. A Roman Catholic "makes up his mind" about sects, and since he considers that Masons belong to a "sect," he feels about us whatever he feels about sects. Therefore, before he meets you or me in person, his mind is already set. In the days of the Anti-Masonic Crusade in the United States, members of the Anti-Masonic party classified our Fraternity among "conspiratorial societies." If he met you and me, such a member would have condemned us in his own mind before knowing us – unlike a court or a judge, he would render a verdict before listening to the testimony. "Conspirators are wicked; Freemasons are conspirators; these two men are Freemasons; therefore, they are wicked." And then (though not to multiply examples unnecessarily), some believe there is a class of associations called secret societies. Their secrets are very odd, and they conclude that Freemasonry is a secret society and, therefore, odd. There is almost no end to the number of "classes" into which associations and societies may be divided or arranged. What a non-Mason thinks or feels about Freemasonry usually is determined by what "class" he believes it belongs to and by what he feels and thinks about that "class."

Where is a man to place Freemasonry? To what kind, sort, or class does it belong? When a man asks these questions in sincerity as one whose only motive is to receive enlightenment, it is a trial to his patience when we Masons give him an answer that must appear to him to be nothing more than a succession of negatives. Freemasonry is not a religion: neither is it a church, nor a handmaiden of religion, nor a school, nor a club, nor a government, nor a political society, nor a conspiracy, nor a secret society, nor a school of occultism, nor a school of mysticism, nor a convivial society, nor a reformation crusade; nor an insurance society, nor a benefit society; nor a benevolent order and is not an association for charity.

These negatives are a positive and affirmative answer to the question because they mean that "Freemasonry is Freemasonry." It can be described and defined only in terms of itself. No generalization consisting of a description, judgment, or appraisal of what a man may take to be a class of social organizations can be true of it because it does not belong to any class of society. No non-Mason, and not even a Candidate, can bring to it a mind already made up about it or bring to bear upon it any set of ideas or judgments previously formed because he has not had any previous experience with what it is. It is self-constituted; it brought itself into existence. What it is has been made by itself. It has grown out of its roots, and it is, therefore, not a specimen of a number of things like itself. No place was ready-made for it to enter, but it has made its place. "What is the place of Freemasonry in the world?" The answer is, "Wherever it is found, there is its place."

When we consider that it has made a place for itself in fifty or more countries and held its place for eight or nine centuries, we must believe that it is worthy of the place it holds in the world.

CHAPTER XXVII
MEMBERS OF WORLDWIDE MASONRY

It is unfortunate that about 1740, we ceased to use the great old Anglo-Saxon word "fellow" as we had always used it before. It meant (and still properly means) a full-fledged member. It meant one who stood on par or on a level with other members, with the same rights, voice, and vote. In Operative Freemasonry, it meant that a young man had completed seven years of apprenticeship and had now become a Master of the Art who could have apprentices of his own, earn wages, have a voice, vote, and have an equal place in the Masonic Community. The Fellowship of Freemasonry consisted of these Fellows. The word is used in its full and original sense in a question which it is the function of this chapter to ask: "A Newly Made Mason has come into fellowship, which means that he is in full-fledged membership. In what fellowship is he? He is a member of what?"

The obvious answer is that he has come into Masonic Fellowship and is a member of Freemasonry. But it is no longer sufficient to give that obvious answer. It is necessary to explain and elaborate upon it because we Masons in the United States are confused and usually mistaken about what it means to be a "member of Freemasonry." We have our Grand Jurisdictions, each walled off from the others and shut up within itself. In some of these Grand Jurisdictions, the local lodges are so little in touch with their Grand Lodge that a member in one of them seldom hears his own Grand Lodge mentioned, and when he does, it is in the form of rumors. In some Jurisdictions, half the lodge members could not name their own Grand Master. If we think of Freemasonry in other countries, we consider it "foreign Masonry." Though the phrase is false in its spirit and mistaken as to its facts, even Grand Lodges use it in their Annual Proceedings. For these reasons, a Newly-Made Mason may begin with the feeling that he is a member of Freemasonry only in the sense of being a member of a local lodge. It is in a tenuous and secondary sense. He is also a member of a Grand jurisdiction, but it is a somewhat disconnected body. As for Freemasonry in other countries, it is "foreign Masonry." It is not American Masonry and therefore is not his affair. It is Canadian Masonry, Mexican Masonry, English, French, or Italian. These various foreign Masonries, he feels, may be interesting, and in some cases, he may be very curious because, after all, foreigners may be quite different. But while he is often curious to hear about them, he feels that they are no concern of his. To such a member Freemasonry means "my lodge."

This idea that when a Candidate is made a Mason, he is thereby made a member of a local lodge only is unfortunate not only because it is a mistake about the facts but also because the Mason who makes the mistake loses that which is largest and best and most wonderful in Freemasonry. To be Raised to the Sublime Degree of Master Mason is to be made a member of the Masonic Fraternity. That Fraternity and World Masonry are the same thing. It is not cut up into separate, national Masonries. Each Mason's fellowship is fellowship in this World Fraternity. It is in it that he holds his membership. No local lodge has a monopoly on his membership, nor can any local lodge cut his Freemasonry down to its own size. How this is true and in what sense it is true can be best explained by going on from one to another of the number of facts about Masonic membership:

1. There is no such thing as "Lodge Masonry." The Masonic Fraternity is a single, indivisible fellowship that is neither divided nor affected by local or national boundaries. Like the sky, it bends a single arch over many countries in which it is at work, and that arch is nowhere broken into separate areas, nor does any country cut it into separate segments. A country is in the Fraternity, but the Fraternity is nowhere shut up inside a country. It has a set of degrees, and a teaching for the world. Masons differ from one country to another; they use different languages and religions, but such differences have nothing to do with their Freemasonry. They all have the hearts of Freemasons. Its only boundaries are the boundaries of the world. The Raising makes a candidate a member of that membership. Only after he has entered it can he petition to become a member of a local lodge. The one World Fraternity is everywhere, the same thing. If it enters any given community to reside and work there, it does so by means of a local lodge. This lodge is the gateway through which a candidate enters the World Fraternity. His membership in that World Fraternity includes his right to be a member in a local lodge, a District, a Grand Jurisdiction, or a Nation. However, these are not separate memberships; they are merely different sides of his one membership. This membership of the World Fraternity is not merely a convenient name for a collection of local or national memberships. It is the only membership there is and includes all secondary memberships. Again, it is not as if a candidate became a local lodge member primarily and then went on to add to it. As being of secondary importance, membership in his Grand Jurisdiction, and then, as a third step, membership in a nation, and as a fourth step, he was to become in some vague and unimportant sense a member of the World Fraternity. It is the other way around, for he becomes a member of the World Fraternity first, and it is not until he does so that he becomes a member of anything

else. A local lodge is the whole of Freemasonry, as it is at work in each local community.

2. Who are Masons? We have a pernicious habit of dividing men and women into types. Our novelists and short story writers do not write about men and women, each of whom is unique, but about a number of types, the businessman type, the rural type, the village type, the artistic type — each writer has a filing cabinet full of types. Our movies are never about any John Smith or Mary Jones — individuals who cannot be duplicated, but about a set of stock characters. What could our illustrators and cartoonists do without these types and stock characters? What could our journalists do? Our preachers? Our politicians?

When in the 1920s, Dr. H. L. Mencken made his onslaught on fraternities, lodges, joiners, etc., he made a type out of them or tried to and called it Rotarian. Freemasons, in Dr. Mencken's eyes, are Rotarians of a more solemn appearance, but they are in other respects a little more comic in his eyes because they dress themselves up in regalia. Why did his ridicule so negatively affect so many American Masons? It was because they secretly agreed with him. Or, instead, when they examined their minds about it, they believed that they had been thinking unconsciously that Freemasonry appeals to men of a *certain type*. They believed that when they had balloted for or against a Petitioner, they had asked themselves whether he would "fit in." In substance, and according to this Mencken notion, men of a certain type naturally gravitate together in a lodge. Any man of that type is already a Mason "in his heart" before he is initiated. What type is he? The "Rotarian," the joiner, the clubable fellow, the backslapper, the "good guy" who calls every man, friend or not, by his first name, etc.

That which shows this Menckenian notion to be false, and which in the long run reduces it to nonsense and absurdity, is the fact that being made a Mason does not mean only membership in a local lodge, which may be a clique of men of similar tastes, but of the World Fraternity. And the membership of the World Fraternity does not contain any stock characters. There is nowhere a *Masonic type*. At that moment when a Candidate becomes a member, he becomes a member alongside Easterners and Westerners, New Englanders and Southerners, Mexicans and Texans, Jews, Mohammedans, Hindus, Chinese, Malayans, sailors, bankers, farmers, loggers, actors, mountaineers, scholars, rich men, poor men, Democrats and Republicans, White men, Black men, Yellow men. When it is said that a candidate becomes a member along with each and every one of those, the words are used in their hardest and most literal sense. Whether near or far, of any station, language, religion, or country, they are his fellow members in the same sense as, and as much as, the men in his local lodge. If anything is true, it is that when a candidate comes into Freemasonry, he comes solely as a man; after he is in it, he is never anything more, less, or other.

3. World Brotherhood is an actuality, not a remote ideal in Masonry. We know snobbishness, race prejudice, and religious prejudices. These, and other, divisions, antipathies, and animosities are so painful and disturbing that justice and human decency demands an end to them. Sadly, many are not Utopian enough to ever expect to see the lion lie down with the lamb, but they would at least like to see the lambs lying down with each other. We are seeing such events.

And what is better still, it cuts both ways; for if a man is too wild with prejudice to work alongside others on whom he has looked down, or whom he hates, and hates because of their color, or religion, or nationality, then he will be, or should be, excluded from Masonic fellowship. If he has entered that fellowship but continues to nourish his prejudices inside his heart, he is a hypocrite, and his lodge, if it knows of it, is hypocritical for permitting him to remain in it. After a man has entered the World Fraternity, it is too late for him to hate any religion, race, or people. It is too late for him to think that he can at least keep them at a distance because Freemasonry does not permit its members to stay at a distance from each other.

4. Freemasonry *Everywhere is Self-Same.* If by any chance a Mason has not yet become wholly a man, if he is cut down in size by narrow-mindedness, or is crippled by sectionalism, or made small by prejudice, he can find no support for himself in the delusion that after all he is an American Mason and need not concern himself with "foreign Masonry." There is no American Masonry; there is only Masonry. It knows of no such word as "foreign." If a Greek or Japanese were to attend his lodge tonight, they would speak in their languages. If I were to attend my lodge, I would speak in English. But what has Freemasonry to do with languages? Sam Houston attended lodge in a tent; Franklin Roosevelt attended lodge in a Masonic Hall of nineteen stories; what have buildings to do with Freemasonry? What difference does it make about the temperature, the costume, the architecture, the food, or the language?

And here again, what we have is not a vague hope, an unattainable ideal, but concrete and actual practices that Freemasons have been carrying on for two hundred years. If a Chicago Mason moves to London, he can visit a lodge or demit to it. If he does, he will follow the same procedure as if he had moved to Detroit. They have Apprentices, Fellowcrafts, and Master Masons in Borneo as they have in Australia. The Masonic tenets are in South Africa the same as in Egypt. Wherever there are regular and duly constituted lodges, any regular Mason will find that their Masonry is the same as the Masonry at home. If in any country there are innovations in the Landmarks, spurious

Masonry, irregular or clandestine lodges, it is the first care of every regular Grand Lodge when in Grand Communication assembled to remedy those problems and to assist regular lodges everywhere to regularize the Masonry of the countries in which they are at work.

In an old tale, it is told of an ancient Greek sage who gained fame because of his profound and incredible wisdom. When a band of men from Crete came to him to bring a Cretan who had been in Hades but had returned, the sage stopped the Cretan: "You need not tell me about Hades; I have been there." When a sailor who had been away for twenty years came to the sage to describe the Antipodes, the sage said, "You need not take my time to tell me about the Antipodes; I have been there." When a neighbor stopped by and burst into tears and began to tell the sage how his little daughter was at the point of death at that very hour, the sage said, "I have been there." Freemasonry has its own profound and incredible wisdom, not because it had been there but because it is there now. It is in all the many lands of this awesome earth. What is there for it yet to learn about them? It has been in war, pestilence, and revolution in every temple, court, and parliament; it has spoken hundreds of languages; it has been in paradise and hell. You belong to it in these ways also, as do I. We are members together in its tolerance and its great wisdom. What we are to do with our membership is up to us.

End of this Cornerstone Book

Thank you for buying this Cornerstone book!

For over 25 years now, we've tried to provide the Masonic community with quality books on Masonic education, philosophy, and general interest. Your support means everything to us and keeps us afloat. Cornerstone is by no means a large company. We are a small family-owned publishing house that depends on your support.

Please visit our website and have a look at the many books we offer as well as the different categories of books.

If your lodge, Grand Lodge, research lodge, book club, or other body would like to have quality Cornerstone books to sell or distribute, write us. We can give you outstanding books, prices, and service.

Thanks again!

Cornerstone Book Publishers
1cornerstonebooks@gmail.com
http://cornerstonepublishers.com

www.ingramcontent.com/pod-product-compliance
Lightning Source LLC
Chambersburg PA
CBHW031123020426
42333CB00012B/200

* 9 7 8 1 6 1 3 4 2 4 0 0 1 *